An Outpouring of Praise for The Write Way

Kay Adams' new book gives you the same profound gifts that Kay brings in person to her journal workshops: Safety, permission, respect, enthusiasm, and as much space as you want to write. Kay is that rare teacher and human being whose expertise is matched by caring and faith in the capacity of an individual to grow. You'll find her superb guidance and faith in these pages, reminding you that you are remarkable, and capable of thriving. This book is just the "write" gift for yourself or someone you love.

> --John Fox CPT, author, *Finding What You Didn't Lose* and *Poetic Medicine*
> Board of Directors, National Association for Poetry Therapy

The Write Way to Wellness melds clinical wisdom and cutting edge research to help the reader deal with stress, trauma and emotional upheaval. In this smart and beautifully organized workbook, Kay Adams guides us through a series of exercises that are both thought-provoking and healing. I strongly recommend this to anyone who is living through a stressful period and who seeks emotional peace.

> --James Pennebaker, author, *Opening Up: The Healing Power of Expressing Emotion*
> Professor of Psychology, University of Texas at Austin

Those of us who study and teach journal writing know that it is a powerful tool for emotional and physical healing. Now Kay Adams has created a much-needed workbook to guide the writer along a gentle, direct path to self-healing.

> --Tristine Rainer, author, *The New Diary* and *Your Life as Story*
> Director, Center for Autobiographical Studies

An exceptionally well-written guide to the healing journey. Through unique and creative writing tools, this workbook will empower those committed to the path of wellness. It covers the whole area of mind-body health, from valuable self-assessment techniques to deeply accessing the Healer Within. I will encourage all my clients to use this to expedite their healing process.

> --Anne L. Day, RN, MA, CMT, HNC, CHTP/I
> Founder, Holistic Nursing professional training program

As we follow life's path into the new millennium we must pack provisions for the journey. *The Write Way to Wellness* is a map for understanding body, mind and spirit. By following the gentle, clear stream of writing exercises, the reader is equipped to make necessary and desired adjustments to life's course. This book is a must for anyone seeking positive change and hope for a healthier future.

> --Dana Reynolds, author, *Be an Angel* and creator, Spiritual Midwifery

The Write Way to Wellness:
A Workbook for Healing and Change

Kathleen Adams, MA LPC

Kathleen Adams

The Center for Journal Therapy
1115 Grant Street, Suite 207
Denver, CO 80203
303-986-6460 • 1-888-421-2298
http://www.journaltherapy.com
E-mail: journaltherapy@aol.com

International Standard Book Number 0-9676552-0-X
Printed in the United States of America

10 9 8 7 6 5 4 3 2

Dedicated to

Sarah Ann Becker
1951-1996

and

Judith K. Mahrer
1934-1996

When it's over, I want to say: All my life
I was a bride married to amazement,
I was the bridegroom, taking the world into my arms.
--Mary Oliver, When Death Comes

The Write Way to Wellness:
A Workbook for Healing and Change

Table of Contents

Acknowledgments

Deep appreciation goes to Dr. James W. Pennebaker and Dr. Joshua M. Smyth and their colleagues, whose groundbreaking research creates a bridge between journal therapy and contemporary medicine.

I am indebted to Anne Day, RN MA CMT CHTP/I, co-creator of the *Journal the Healing Journey* workshop, and to Mary Maynard, RN CHTP, my partner in The Center for Healing and Change, for their many years of friendship, and for their steadfast vision of what it means to be a healer.

Thanks to Christine Testolini, the answer to prayer, whose wisdom, guidance and expertise made my first venture into self-publishing both empowering and fun; Barbara Barstow, who handles the roles of Muse and business manager with equal aplomb; Michele Craig, who beautifully translated the concept of this book into design; Scott Laudenslager and Kimco Printing for excellence and intelligence at all stages of production; and Jonathan Goldman, who provided healing background music for the accompanying meditation tape.

Angie Pincin of Pincin & Prior Coaching tilled a fertile ground for the seeds of this project to take root, and I am grateful for her clarity and vision.

It is a joy to be associated with my extraordinary colleagues at Foothills Healing Arts Center in Lakewood, Colorado, as fine a collection of visionaries and healers as can be found under one roof. I also extend appreciation to my colleagues in the National Association for Poetry Therapy, particularly my mentors, Dr. Peggy Osna Heller and Dr. Kenneth Gorelick.

Since 1994 I have had the opportunity and privilege to lead journal therapy groups for people with HIV/AIDS at Denver Health Medical Center. Much of what I know of writing and wellness has come from the struggles and triumphs of these men and women, and I am profoundly grateful for the opportunity to be both teacher and student. I also extend heartfelt thanks to my co-facilitators, Mary Ann Bolkovatz, RN MS; Sher Sauvé, RN MS; and Joyce Kobayashi, MD, who have championed The Writing Group at every stage, and who model true compassion.

I am ever grateful for The Center for Journal Therapy's worldwide community of Certified Instructors, students, clients and friends. Thank you for your encouragement, loyalty, support and commitment to healing yourselves and others through writing.

Love and hugs to my big, noisy, wonderful family for cheerfully loving me through the eccentricities and idiosyncrasies of the writing life, and to my extended sisterhood, Marta Hedde, Dale Wenglowski, Dana Reynolds, Jean Jameson, Andrea Hilgert and Thia Walser, for walking the path with me.

Finally, and always, I am thankful for the grace and guidance of the Divine.

Introduction

How will writing help heal this person or circumstance? I have sat for thirty thousand hours with people and their journals, and this is the constant question I ask myself. That writing *does* heal is unmistakable. It is not possible to be in the presence of those who write their way through moments of ecstasy and moments of despair, critical illness and crucial life choice, spiritual awakening and free-falls into the Mystery, without acknowledgment of the truth that writing heals.

My gift as a journal therapist -- one who facilitates healing of body, psyche and soul through the pathway of writing -- is to offer the right question, invite the right life story, suggest the right technique, evoke the right image that will enhance the opportunity for healing.

That's what this workbook offers you: A carefully chosen, well-crafted series of questions, story invitations, techniques and evocations that will place your feet on a healing path. The very best suggestion I can offer you is to co-author this book with me by actually writing in it. Make it your own. Make it your conduit for healing energy, your own mind/body laboratory, a map of your wellness journey. Use it up. Don't worry about whether you'll want these forms or worksheets again; there are blank ones at the back specifically to be photocopied and used over and over. Don't worry that your handwriting will be messy, or that you'll misspell words. Who cares? If you can read it, that's all that matters. No one is grading or judging you here. This is your book. This is your body. This is your health.

There are two exceptions to the suggestion that you actually write in this book. One is if you truly prefer writing on a keyboard. If that's the case, then prop the book beside you and type instead of write. If you want, you can print out your writing, trim it to fit, and tape or glue it onto the pages of the book.

The other exception is if you run into a process or exercise that has no interest or appeal for you, or that seems too difficult, time-consuming or overwhelming. Rather than interrupt your momentum, just move on. Come back to it later. Or don't. Just skip it entirely.

This workbook is designed to operate on two levels. In the moment, you are going through a process of discovery about your own healing journey. But you are also learning valuable, tested, tried-and-true journal techniques that can be used over and over again. The work doesn't end when the workbook does. You can take the techniques you have practiced and learned -- Dialogues, AlphaPoems, Lists, Sentence Stems, Questions, Clustering, Captured Moments, Structured Writes, Sprints -- as well as the concepts of the Healthy Self, the Inner Healer, the Balance Wheel, and all the rest, and use them in an ongoing journal of your life.

If you are concerned about privacy, address your concerns head-on. Tell the people in your household that this book isn't for anyone's eyes but your own. Ask them to respect your privacy. Then keep the workbook with you, in a bookbag, briefcase or desk drawer. You have a right to privacy. You don't have to share this with anyone you don't want to share it with.

Aside from this workbook and your favorite writing instruments, the only supplies you'll need for this journey are simple art materials (crayons, colored pencils or felt-tip markers), a package of foil stick-on stars (the kind we got on our homework when we were in elementary school) and a blank notebook or journal to contain any "overflow" you might have from these pages — and to continue your journal journey when the workbook is complete. These materials are available at most office supply stores or grocery stores. Have them handy early on so that you won't have to interrupt yourself when you get to the parts that require them. The instructions for your Health History in Section 3 suggest that you write in two different colors of ink pen, preferably contrasting, so you'll want to round up a second color of pen before you get there.

I invite you to commit to this workbook as a process. It certainly isn't necessary to write every day, but it may be helpful to segregate the sections into one-week units. Depending on how you treat the four consecutive daily writes in Section 1 (as stand-alone or as supplement to Section 2), you would be complete in eight or nine weeks.

This work is exceptionally powerful when it is done in a facilitated group setting. If you are part of a support group or wellness community, suggest a *Write Way to Wellness* curriculum. Call us at The Center for Journal Therapy for questions, or if you'd like to bring in an outside facilitator. Many of our Certified Instructors are Wellness Specialists.

A companion audiotape of entrance meditations is available for the guided imageries in this workbook. Meditations available on tape are marked throughout. Ordering information is on page 155.

With the new medical research showing a demonstrated correlation between writing and healing, The Center for Journal Therapy's mission statement, *To make the healing art of reflective writing accessible to all who desire self-directed change,* has never been more relevant. Whether you are seeking healing for a specific ailment or expanding the good health you already have, this user-friendly guide will lead you along your own journey to optimum wellness.

Kathleen Adams, MA LPC
Director, The Center for Journal Therapy
Denver, Colorado
www.journaltherapy.com

A Note to Health Care/Helping Professionals

The Write Way to Wellness was written in response to an outpouring of requests from people in all stages of wellness and disease, and their health care/helping professionals, for immediately applicable skills in the use of journal writing as a tool for holistic health and wellness.

If you intend to use this material with your clients, I strongly encourage you to complete the workbook yourself. You will be able to more appropriately help your clients if you have first-hand experience with the techniques and processes.

This work is extremely powerful when done in group settings. I suggest an 8-week curriculum based on Sections 2-9. Section 1 can be assigned as homework in the first week. If you would like to bring in an outside facilitator, contact The Center for Journal Therapy. Our Instructor Certification Training has prepared dozens of people around the United States and Canada. If you would like training as a facilitator, please call.

Journal therapists are professionally associated through the National Association for Poetry Therapy (NAPT). If you are using journals in your work with your clients, I encourage you to consider membership in this fine interdisciplinary organization. NAPT's worldwide membership is approximately equally divided among psychotherapy/mental health professionals; medical/health care professionals; educators/librarians; and poets/writers/lovers of words. Credentialing in both developmental and clinical poetry/journal therapy is offered through NAPT. See page 153 for more information.

This workbook is loosely modeled after *Journal the Healing Journey,* a continuing education workshop I co-created with my colleague Anne L. Day, designed to teach these processes and techniques to registered nurses, counselors, and other healing/helping professionals. If you are interested in approved continuing education trainings, let us know.

I am very interested in your feedback, suggestions, experiences and questions about this work. Please call, write or e-mail.

This is the private workbook of

_____
(your name here)

begun on _____
(date)

and completed on _____
(date)

Please do not read without first asking permission!
Thank you for your respect.

Section One

One Hour to Better Health

One Hour to Better Health

In the 1980s Dr. James W. Pennebaker, a research psychologist, studied the impact of cathartic writing on health. He asked subjects to write for only 15-20 minutes a day, for four consecutive days, about emotionally difficult topics. At the end of the study, he discovered that his subjects showed physiological changes that correlated to increased immune system functioning. These positive changes lasted up to six weeks after the end of the four-day writing experiment! And even months later, subjects reported fewer visits to health clinics and medical doctors for stress-related illnesses.

A decade later, in 1996-97, Dr. Joshua Smyth and colleagues replicated this study with rheumatoid arthritis and asthma sufferers. Subjects were asked to write about "the most stressful event of their lives" for only three days, 20 minutes per day. Four months later, there was "clinically significant" improvement in nearly 50% of the cases! "This is the first study to demonstrate that writing about stressful life experiences improves physician ratings of disease severity in chronically ill patients," writes Dr. Smyth in the April 14, 1999 issue of the *Journal of the American Medical Association (JAMA).* Psychiatrist David Spiegel, MD comments in an editorial published in the same issue of *JAMA,* "Were the authors to have provided similar outcome evidence about a new drug, it likely would be in widespread use within a short time.... (T)he authors have provided evidence that medical treatment is more effective when standard pharmacological intervention is combined with the management of emotional distress."

This groundbreaking research gives us clear and compelling reason to believe that writing in a journal or diary does more than simply chronicle thoughts and feelings, or record them for the future. There are actual healing benefits. But *how* does writing heal?

According to Dr. Pennebaker, the psychological state of *inhibition* — holding things back, or in, rather than giving them expression — is hard physiological work. "Active inhibition," he says, "means that people must consciously restrain, hold back, or in some way exert effort to *not* think, feel or behave."

On the other hand, says Dr. Pennebaker, *confrontation* — actively talking *or writing* about emotionally difficult experiences — offers welcome physiological and psychological release, and "the biological stress of inhibition is immediately reduced."

Additionally, giving form to difficult emotional experiences through words and language offers a context and a container. Understanding, insight and meaning all begin with naming and describing — with telling ourselves the truth about what we have experienced, and how we feel about it. That's what this four-day process helps you do.

So let's begin at the beginning. Let's start with four consecutive days of timed writings, following the guidelines that Dr. Pennebaker suggests.

Dr. Pennebaker's Guidelines
for Emotional Release Writing

1. **Choose an experience** that is emotionally difficult for you and that you have a hard time talking or maybe even thinking about. It can be from any time in your life — childhood, adolescence, early adulthood, or something more recent. It might even be something that you are experiencing right now.

2. **Tell yourself a story** in which you describe both the experience and your feelings about it. Don't hold back.

3. **Don't worry about details.** Spelling, grammar and punctuation aren't important. It's also less important to get all the factual details correct than it is to stay true to the emotional experience.

4. **Write for about 15 or 20 minutes.** Write without stopping, and without re-reading, until the time has passed. If you need a little more time to bring the story to a stopping place, give yourself a few more minutes. Try to write continuously.

5. **Do this for four consecutive days.** You may write about the same event more than once, allowing yourself to continue the story or deepen into it each time, or you may choose different topics. And it isn't always necessary to write about terrible events — anything that you have a hard time talking about will be useful for this purpose.

6. **If you write about the same event all four days,** the second and third days might address how this incident or experience has impacted your current situation. How did it shape you? How does it affect how your life has evolved? What impact has it had on your love life, work life, family life, and so on?

7. **Notice your feelings as and after you write.** It may be that you'll feel upset or distressed immediately after this writing. Dr. Pennebaker's research subjects reported that these feelings usually only lasted about an hour, although in rare cases they lasted a day or two.

Adapted from *Opening Up: The Healing Power of Expressing Emotions* by James W. Pennebaker (paperback edition, 1997, Guilford Press) and from conversations with Dr. Pennebaker.

As a journal therapist who has specialized in using writing as a treatment of traumatic stress, I can tell you that the structure and containment of this method reduces the possibility of emotional overload. If, however, you are working with very difficult material (for instance, sexual or physical trauma from childhood that you have never allowed yourself to think or talk about before), and you find that you are having intrusive symptoms such as flashbacks, nightmares or "out-of-body" feelings, then discontinue this process and move on to some of the other exercises in this workbook. If the symptoms persist even after you have stopped writing about them directly, then consider seeking help from a reputable counselor or psychotherapist.

You needn't postpone working with the rest of the ideas and exercises in this workbook while you spend the first four days on the research model. Feel free to continue following the guidance in the remainder of the workbook while you do this four-day process. In fact, you may find that doing so helps soothe and balance any residual feelings of upset you may experience from writing about stressful events.

Write for 15-20 minutes about an experience that was emotionally difficult for you, and that you've had a hard time thinking or talking about. It can be from any time in your life. Tell both
    (a) the story of what happened, and
    (b) your feelings at the time.
Write quickly, continuously and without re-reading. Don't worry about spelling or grammar. Continue on the white space on this page, or additional sheets of paper, if necessary.

 # Day One

Today's Date _____   Start Time _____   End Time _____

Again, write for 15-20 minutes about an experience that was emotionally difficult for you and that is difficult to talk or think about. It can be the same topic as yesterday, or a new one. Tell both the story and how you felt about it. Write quickly, continuously and without re-reading. Don't worry about spelling or grammar. Use the white space of this page to continue if necessary, or add extra paper.

 **Day Two**

Today's Date _____   Start Time _____   End Time _____

Again today, write for 15-20 minutes, telling both the story of a difficult or stressful experience, and your feelings at the time. If you are writing about the same story, see if you can deepen into it by telling another aspect or layer of it. Since tomorrow is the last day of this four-day write, you may want to think about starting to tie things up. By now you're getting used to writing quickly and continuously, and not worrying about spelling and grammar. You've also figured out what to do if you need more space to write.

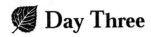 # Day Three

Today's Date _____   Start Time _____   End Time _____

This is the last day of writing for 15-20 minutes about an emotionally difficult or stressful experience. Tie things up today, bringing to a close the story and your feelings about it, and perhaps explore how this event or experience fits into the overall context of your life — who you were then, who you are now, and who you are becoming.

When you have finished today's write, turn the page and jot down some of your awarenesses and impressions about this process.

 # Day Four

Today's Date _____ Start Time _____ End Time _____

Re-read what you have written over four days about your stressful or difficult life experiences, and the emotions you associate with them. How do you feel, now that these stories are off your chest? What are you aware of? Can you see any connections between these stories and any other aspects of your life, as you are living it today? What, if anything, do you understand differently? What's interesting about this?

You might explore these awarenesses using one or more of these starter phrases:

As I re-read these stories, I am aware of....
            .... I notice that.....
            ... I am surprised by.....
            ....I am curious about....
            ....I feel....

🍃 Review and Synthesize

Today's Date _____   Start Time _____   End Time _____

Section Two

Getting Started

Reflect on these thoughts on the connection between writing and healing. Space is left after each one so that you can personalize your own responses to each idea. How important is this reason to you? How might your wellness journey be enhanced by this suggestion?

❧ Ten Reasons Why Journal Writing is a Powerful Ally in Healing

1. **Immediacy and availability.** A journal is available at 3 a.m., during a migraine, in the doctor's waiting room, when no one on your support list is home. A journal's immediacy lessens the need to rely on the kindness of strangers or the patience of health care professionals, family and friends.

Describe some of the times when you've desperately wished you had someone to talk to.

2. **Catharsis and insight.** The important work of healing often brings with it a host of perfectly normal, but difficult, feelings — anger, fear, despair, frustration. Your journal absorbs these feelings without judgment, censure or reprisal, and the insight gained from catharsis is an important step in healing.

What feelings are the most difficult for you in the healing journey? Would you be able to write about them?

3. **Unconditional acceptance and silent friend.** As one journalkeeper said, "My journal has become the archetypal friend. I have used and abused it more than any person would have tolerated. But it was always there waiting for me, totally accepting, totally present. I could ignore it, discount its value, and it never took offense. I never had to start over. I never had to apologize. What a blessed gift!"

Where in your life do you receive the gift of unconditional acceptance and total presence? Could you use more of this?

4. **Observe health-enhancing cycles and patterns.** Our habitual behaviors either promote wellness or contribute to discomfort and disease. Observing behaviors through charts, logs or reflections offers valuable data that can be used to maximize wellness.

Which of your habits promote wellness? Which contribute to discomfort or disease?

5. **Get to know different parts of yourself.** Learning to listen to and communicate with your bodymind, Inner Healer, Healthy Self and other energetic aspects of the Self is one of the great gifts of journalkeeping.

Are you in touch with the different aspects of yourself? If so, how do you connect? If not, how might these aspects of self help you in your journey toward wellness?

6. **Strengthen intuition and inner guidance.** It is simply amazing how much wisdom we hold within us, and how reliably we can access it just by turning inward, asking sincere questions, listening, and writing down what we hear.

To what extent are you in touch with, and do you rely on, intuition and inner guidance?

7. **Expand creativity.** Once initial discomfort and resistance to writing is overcome, nearly every journalkeeper finds that writing can be a reassuring, nurturing, safe creative outlet for thoughts and feelings. This increased flexibility with the creative process often leads to spontaneous brainstorming of options and choices for wellness.

How do you express your creativity?

8. **Self-empowerment and self-esteem.** Journal writing encourages self-reliance and self-responsibility. The healing journey is literally mapped out, one page at a time, and the accumulation of life experience and wisdom adds up to the recognition that we are, in fact, the predominant creative forces in our own lives.

How do you empower yourself in your healing journey?

9. **Release past hurts and judgments.** Holding on to the past is a surefire energy drain. Resentment, guilt, blame and bottled-up grief block access to the Healer Within. The safe container of your journal receives it all, filling up and becoming more in the process, and prepares you to release old wounds and extend forgiveness to yourself and others.

What past hurts and judgments would you like to release and forgive?

10. **Witness to healing.** The journal provides an ongoing record of the healing journey. Months and years down the road, you can look at past volumes to assure yourself that you *are* making progress, you *do* master wellness principles, you *can* heal.

Who is the Healthy Self you are becoming?

Aside from the strong suggestion to date every entry, there are no "rules" to journal writing. However, a few simple practices will ground your writing and help it grow strong and hardy, without frustration, struggle and difficulty. Try sinking these practices deeply, like roots, and you'll dramatically increase your satisfaction and results.

Eight Ways to Ground Your Writing

1. **Permission.** Forget everything you think you "should" do if you're going to write a journal. You don't have to write every day, or in complete sentences, or in properly spelled and punctuated language. Your handwriting can be messy, your thoughts unclear, and you can quit whenever you want. Lighten up! Give yourself permission to write in whatever way best fits your mood, style, or momentary inclination.

What if I gave myself permission to write without limits?

2. **Balance.** Journals without balance are like bicycles with leaky tires: Any momentum that is built up is quickly depleted. Remedy: If your writing is out of balance, consciously seek the opposite polarity If you never write about feelings, start naming the "feeling du jour" and jotting down a few thoughts and observations about it. If you always write about high drama, try capturing a moment of serenity. If you notice your writing is filled with complaints and frustrations, stop and make a list of things you are grateful for.

Where might I notice that I'm out of balance?

3. **Privacy.** Respect privacy and boundaries — your own, and those of others. Leave the first page of any new notebook or journal blank, so that there is a discreet barrier between your private thoughts and someone else's eyes. Protect your privacy by keeping your journal in its own special place, whether that is a nightstand drawer, a briefcase, a locked filing cabinet or a password-protected computer program. And extend these same privacy privileges to others. Don't read anyone else's journal without their express invitation.

Do I have privacy concerns? If so, how might I proactively manage them?

4. Honesty. Don't be afraid of your own truth. The more honestly and deeply you are able to write, the more healing benefit you will receive.

How honest can I be with myself? Am I willing to be tell myself the truth?

5. Silence. Honor journal silence. It can be a valuable messenger. It does *not* automatically mean you are "failing" at keeping a journal if it falls silent for days, weeks or even months at a time. Know that you can always come back and pick up where you left off.

Have I ever quit writing a journal, and decided this meant that I wasn't doing it right?

6. Attention. Pay attention to the subtle differences that begin to emerge and reveal themselves as you write your healing journey. Noting them allows you to find connections and bridges between your inner and outer worlds.

How much attention do I pay to my inner experience?

7. **Structure.** When you write, you are moving thoughts, feelings and energy out of your mind and body and into a neutral, receptive place where they are safely stored. This can feel unpredictable, unboundaried and even frightening without some simple foundations and structures. Set limits and stay with them. Write for only ten minutes, or stop when you feel fatigued, or stand up and stretch in the middle of a write.

Where in my life do I appreciate structure and form? How can I transfer these habits or techniques to the journal experience?

8. **Reflection.** Before you begin to write, develop the habit of closing your eyes, taking a few deep breaths, and turning your attention inward. And at the end of each writing session, harvest the learning by re-reading what you've written and reflect on what you notice, how you feel, what action steps you might take. This takes just a few extra minutes and provides valuable pathways.

What have I learned from this process, so far? How does it feel to be answering these questions? What am I noticing about myself?

Bread for the Journey

This is a list of the most enduring and sustaining journal techniques — different ways to write that offer consistent and reliable results. You'll be coached through many of these techniques in this workbook. Experiment with the others on your own. All of these techniques are covered in detail in my other books, *Journal to the Self* (1990, Warner Books) and *The Way of the Journal, 2nd Ed* (1998, Sidran Press).

AlphaPoem. A perennial favorite. Write the alphabet, A-Z (or any other collection of letters) vertically down the side of a page. Then write a poem in which each successive line begins with the next letter.

Artmaking. Gives form, shape and color to personal symbolism, emotions, attitudes and thoughts. Keep simple materials such as crayons, felt-tip markers or colored pencils, accessible.

Captured Moments. Vignettes capturing the sensations of particularly meaningful or emotional experiences. Written from the senses with strong descriptions. Usually only one or two paragraphs.

Character Sketch. A written portrait of another person or of a part of the self.

Clustering. Also called mind-mapping or webbing. Clustering is visual free association around a central word or phrase. Lines and circles connect key thoughts and associations to the central core. A brief writing to synthesize findings may follow.

Community Journal. An ongoing communication book kept interactively with family members, caregivers or housemates.

Dialogue. An imaginary conversation written in two or more voices. On the page, it looks like a movie or play script.

Dreamwork. Writing down dreams is the first step to journal dreamwork. From there, any number of techniques can be used for self-interpretation.

Five- or Ten-Minute Writing Sprints. Timed writes designed to bring focus and intensity in short bursts.

Free Write (Stream of Consciousness). This unstructured, unboundaried, free-form narrative writing starts anywhere and goes where it pleases. Although it is the default technique for most journal writers, it is not necessarily the most effective. If you find yourself pulling away from your journal because your free writes feel disturbing or distressing, try a different technique, perhaps one with more structure — a Sprint, or a List, or a Structured Write.

Inner Wisdom/Inner Healer. A way to reliably connect with that "still, small voice" that speaks truth when we turn within.

Lists. Staccato, linear organization of thoughts, ideas, tasks.

Lists of 100. A list on a predetermined theme or topic with 100 entries, some or many of which are likely to be repetitions.

Perspectives. An alteration in point of view that provides a different perspective on an event or a situation. For instance, you may write from a point in time in the past or the future, actually dating your page with a different month and/or year. Or you may write in the voice of someone or something else, as if he/she/it were writing in his/her/its journal about *you*.

Sentence Stem. A sentence completion process. Fill in the blank with a word or phrase. A gentle and safe way to get started writing about a difficult issue.

Springboard. A topic sentence or question written at the beginning of a journal entry to help focus and clarify the writing, usually followed by a Free Write or Writing Sprint. As a general rule, Springboards written as statements or Sentence Stems seem to stimulate thoughts and opinions, whereas Springboards written as questions tend to stimulate feelings and wonderings.

Structured Write. A series of Sentence Stems, grouped and sequenced to reveal consistently deepening layers of information and awareness. The basic formula goes like this (write 1-2 sentences on each):
1) I want to explore—; 2) The first thing that comes to mind—; 3) Beneath the surface I find—;
4) I'm disturbed or uncomfortable with—; 5) I feel hopeful about—; 6) I would benefit from—;
7) My next step is—.

Unsent Letter. Besides Free Writing, the most common journal technique. A metaphoric communication to another that is written with the specific intention that it will not be shared with the designated audience.

A Journey Through the Body*

Read through this meditation. Then, if you are alone, read it again to yourself, closing your eyes and following its guidance between sections. Stay as long as you like in each area of the body. This meditation may take 10 or 15 minutes to fully complete, so give yourself plenty of time.

If you have someone available to slowly read the meditation to you, that's even better.
If you're ambitious, you could even read it into a tape recorder, and play it back for yourself.
When you are complete with the meditation you will need crayons, colored pencils or markers, so please have those ready before you begin.

Settle into a comfortable position in your chair. Loosen any tight clothing.
Take a moment to notice your breathing. Don't change it. Just notice it.

We're going to take a journey through your body. Imagine that your attention is a sensor with exploratory feelers or antenna that will reach into each part of your body, every limb and organ. There is no need to change anything. Simply be curious and alert. Awareness may come in many forms:
  As sensations of pain, fatigue, soreness, tightness, relaxation, tenderness, openness.
  As colors, shapes, textures, temperatures.
  As images, symbols, pictures.
  As emotional feelings of fear, anxiety, shame, anger, pride, gratitude, appreciation.
  As markers of injury or disease, healing or wellness.

Now, turn your attention to your feet, beginning with the soles of your feet. Notice if there is any pain or tension or soreness in your feet. Notice if your feet feel fine. Wiggle your toes. Rotate your ankles. Notice how your feet are feeling.

Now move your awareness into the calves of your legs. Allow your awareness to explore the muscles, bones, ligaments, nerves, blood and cells of your calves. Notice any sensations, feelings or images that you associate with your calves. Notice your skin.

When you are ready, move your awareness into your knees. Explore your knee joints, noticing any sensations, images or awarenesses that come from your knees.

Now your thighs and upper legs. Take as much time as you need.

When you are ready, shift your awareness to your hips, your hip sockets, and your sacrum. Notice your sitbones, where your buttocks meet the chair. Send awareness into your tailbone, the base of your spine.

Now turn your attention to your pelvic area. Turn your focus inward to your colon, your large intestines, your reproductive organs. Move your awareness to your genitals and buttocks. Notice your lumbar spine. This is a busy, full part of your body. Allow yourself to notice differences in feeling between different parts of your pelvic region. Take your time.

When you are ready, move to your abdominal area. Feel inside for your stomach, liver, kidneys, pancreas, gall bladder, spleen, small intestines. Notice your waist and tummy. Feel your spine, ribs, muscles.

*Meditation available on audio tape.

Now move your awareness into your chest area. Feel your heart, lungs, breasts, back, spine, muscles, ligaments. Feel your sternum, clavicle, shoulders. Allow your awareness to follow any sensations in your chest and upper back. Feel your skin.

Notice your shoulders. Rotate your shoulder cuffs. Follow your awareness down your arms, through the upper arms, into the elbows. Notice if there are sensations in your joints, in your forearms, wrists, hands. Flex your fingers, if you comfortably can. Notice any feelings, images or awarenesses in your arms.

Go back to your shoulders. Feel the places where your shoulders connect with your spine, and where your spine connects with your head. Experience the broad muscles that crisscross your back and shoulders. Gently rotate your neck.

When you are ready, turn your attention to your head. Feel your face. Travel inside your ears, through your mouth, down your throat. Explore your teeth and tongue. Drop your jaw and rotate it.

Notice your nose. Inhale as deeply as you comfortably can. Follow your breath. Feel your sinuses. Explore your eyes. The skin on your face, neck and scalp Your hair. Go inside and focus on your brain.

Now, when you have moved completely from your toes to your head, bring your awareness to yourself as a complete body, skin and bones and muscle, organs and tissue, blood and air and water, cells and nerves, a brain that regulates the miracle that is your body.

Notice any feelings, images, sensations that arise When you are ready, **turn the page and continue with the next** *stage of this exercise.*

On the following page are body drawings. Use colored pencils, markers or crayons to create a self-portrait that represents your experience of your body from the guided meditation.

When you are complete, use the space around the drawing, or the white space on this page, to make notes to yourself about the journey through your body.

My Self-Portrait

Today's Date _____   Start Time _____   End Time _____

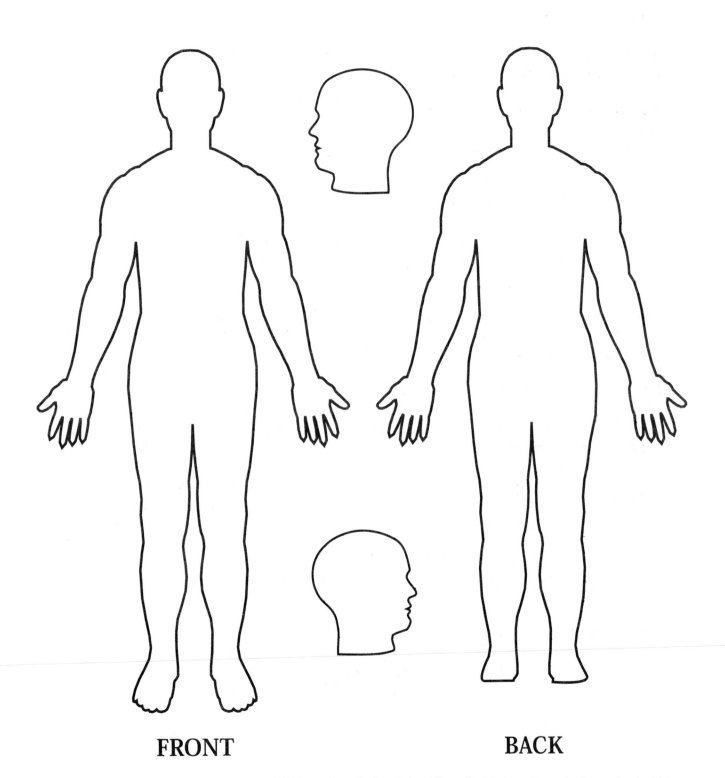

FRONT   **BACK**

The Dialogue technique is one of the most reliable journal devices.
It is the Swiss army knife of the journal toolbox because it is so versatile and handy.

It is a way of giving voice to the wisdom inside yourself.

A journal Dialogue is a written conversation in which you write both parts.
On the page, it looks like a movie or play script.

You can dialogue with just about anyone or anything.
We're going to do a Dialogue with the Body.
Here is an example from someone whose Body sounds quite assertive:

> Me: Body, why can't we shake this cold?
> *Body: Spend one entire 24-hour day in bed, then ask me again.*
> Me: But I can't afford to take a day off.
> *Body: Can you afford NOT to? How long will this go on,*
> *you feeling at half-capacity, if you don't listen to what I say?*
> *Give me a chance to heal!*

Don't worry if your Dialogue doesn't sound like this one. It probably won't.
Your Dialogue partners will have their own personalities, too. Part of the fun and wonder of this process is discovering their "voices."

When you are writing a Dialogue, remember:
Either of you may ask any question and receive an honest answer.
Either of you may make any statement or express any opinion and know it will be heard without judgment, blame or criticism.

Before you begin, look at the self-portrait you drew. What aspect of your body do you want to "talk" with? Perhaps it is a particular body part or organ, or an illness, or a feeling. Choose some aspect of your body to Dialogue with.

We'll come back to Dialogue in another section. For now, just ask your Body a few questions*. If you want to continue, of course, you can do so on the back side of the page, or in the white spaces surrounding it.

Here are some questions you might ask:
> *Body, what are you trying to tell me?*
> *What do you want and need from me?*
> *What are some actions I can take that will increase health and wellness?*

*Meditation available on audio tape.

🍃 Dialogue with the Body

Me:

Body:

Me:

Body:

Me:

Body:

Section Three

Your Current Reality

A wise man once said,
"If you don't know where you're going, you'll probably end up someplace else."

Similarly, if you don't know where you're starting from, you might not recognize that you're making progress.

So let's spend some time assessing your current reality. Who you are. How you're feeling. And how you got here.

Here are three good questions to begin our journey.

🌿 *Who am I?*
How do I describe or introduce myself?
What are the roles I wear?
And who am I behind and underneath the roles?

🌿 *Why am I here?*
What brings me to this journey?
What motivates me to begin this exploration?
Why this workbook, at this time?

🌿 *What do I want?*
What are my desires and dreams?
If I could achieve specific goals and outcomes related to my health, what would they be?
What do I value?
What matters to me?

Who Am I?
Why Am I Here?
What Do I Want?

I am......

I am here because......

I want.....

For this process you will need two different colored ink pens, preferably with contrast — red and either black or blue work well.

Use the diagram on the next page to create your lifetime health history.
(If you are over age 70, use the white space on this page to extend your health lines.)
You may want to complete your health history chronologically, like a story that begins with your birth and continues through the decades. Or you may prefer to let the entries spill all over the page as you think of them. Either way is fine. But use different colors for your challenges and your improvements.

In the space below each half-decade, note any significant challenges to your health.
Did you have a difficult birth? Childhood illnesses? Broken arms or legs?
Sports injuries? Chronic ailments, such as asthma or allergies?
Surgeries? Illnesses? Infertility? Difficult pregnancies? Miscarriages?
Weight gain or loss? Hypertension? Heart problems?
Trauma through violence, combat, accident? Sexual trauma? Injuries?
Cancer? Problems with prostate or menopause? Depression? Anxiety? Traumatic grief?
Hearing problems? Dental problems? Eye problems?
Difficulties with joints or movement? High-risk behaviors?
Immune system problems? Kidney? Colon? Liver? Recurrent infections?
Alcoholism or drug dependency? Eating too much or too little, or purging?
Long-term chronic illness? Life-threatening illness?
List significant health challenges, from birth to the present moment.

In the second color, note significant improvements to your health.
Fitness programs? Successful weight management? Lowered blood pressure?
Successful surgeries? Corrected vision, dental, hearing loss?
Illnesses that responded to medication or treatment? Hospitalizations?
Healthy pregnancies and births? Lifestyle changes? Management through medication?
Sports activities? Quitting smoking or drinking?
Injuries that healed? Episodes of physical therapy or rehabilitation?
Psychotherapy or counseling? Nutrition? Wellness orientation?
List the significant things that have improved your health, from birth to the present moment.

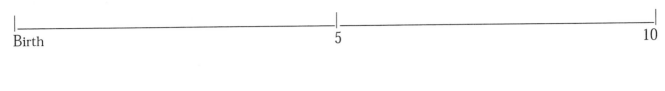

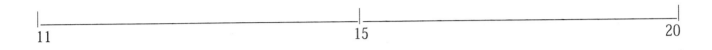

Birth   5   10

11   15   20

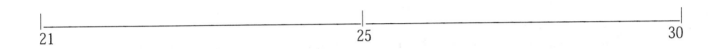

21   25   30

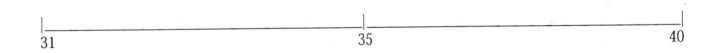

31   35   40

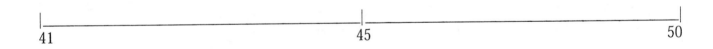

41   45   50

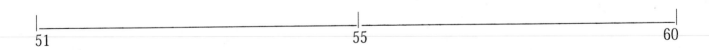

51   55   60

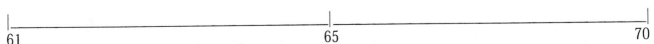

61   65   70

Now, stand back and review your Health History. Synthesize your findings. Some points to consider:

Are there periods in your life where you have constellations of illness, injury or healing?
Who or what influenced you most during your healing episodes?
Which of your health challenges are completely in your past? What healed you?
Compared to where you have been in the past, how is your current state of health?
As you review your Health History, what else are you aware of? What else do you notice?
Are there any surprises here?
How do you feel as you review your Health History, from birth to the present moment?

Review and Synthesize

Today's Date _____   Start Time _____   End Time _____

Clustering is an excellent journal technique to use when you want to gather a lot of diverse information very quickly. Clustering is sometimes called "mind mapping" because it gives you a visual map of your thought process.

Clustering is very simple to do. Just start with a central word or phrase in the middle of the page, and build a web of thoughts, ideas, associations and feelings. Go as far out as you can, then return to the center. You can add new clusters at any time.

On the facing page, Cluster the gifts and challenges about your current reality. Begin with the circles provided, then add your own. When you're finished, look at the entire page as if it were a map. Write what you notice in the white space below.

What I notice about my Current Reality Cluster is......

🍃 Current Reality Cluster

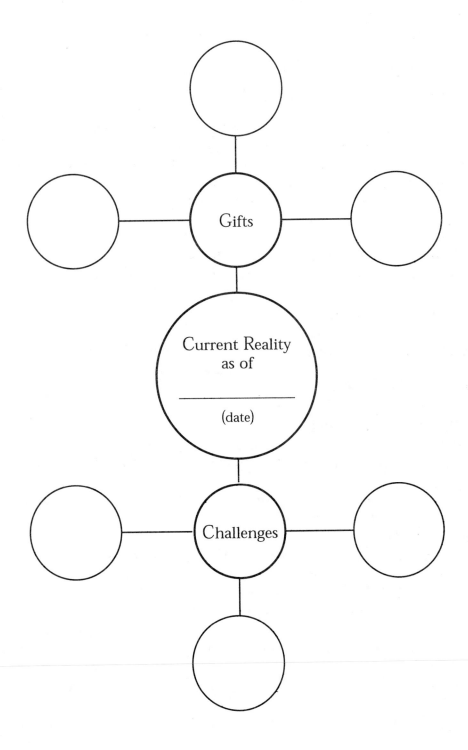

The Relaxation Response is a simple, specific form of bodily calm developed by Dr. Herbert Benson, who teaches at the Harvard Medical School and has founded the Mind/Body Medical Institute there. The state evoked is the opposite of the stress-related "fight-or-flight" reaction. With the Relaxation Response, blood pressure is lowered, heart rate is decreased, breathing is deepened, fears are lessened, anxieties are eased, and inner calm and strength are activated.

There are two basic components to the Relaxation Response:

- Choose a focus word, phrase or movement that has a soothing, inspirational, optimistic or comforting effect on you. If you are connected to a religious or spiritual faith, the focus might be a word, phrase or prayer from your doctrine. If you prefer a secular focus, you might choose a word such as *peace.... oneness.... calm.... love.... rainbow.... hope.... sunrise.... nature.... beauty....* Once you have chosen your word(s), use the same one(s) each time you do the Relaxation Response. Hold the focus as you sit or lie comfortably, with your eyes closed and your breathing deep and rhythmic. Repeat your focus word(s) silently to yourself. Concentrate your attention on the repetition and any images that arise.

- When other thoughts or ideas come into your mind, *passively disregard* them and return to your focus word(s). Do not attempt to shove intrusive thoughts from your mind, and don't try to not think about them. Simply.... do nothing. Ignore them. Return to your focus word(s) and the images conjured. Return to the repetition.

That's all. Simple, isn't it? And surprisingly effective!

Invoking the Relaxation Response*
- Find a comfortable position.
- Begin to breathe deeply and slowly.
- Relax your muscles.
- Place your attention on your focus word(s). Breathe your focus in and out. Allow images to arise.
- When other thoughts come in, simply disregard them. Return to your focus. Repeat your word(s) and enjoy the images that arise.
- Continue for 10-20 minutes.
- When you are ready to return, allow yourself a minute or two of transition. Sit or lie quietly, with your eyes closed, allowing other thoughts to return. Then slowly and carefully open your eyes and bring yourself back to current reality.
- Repeat this as often as you'd like, but optimally at least once a day.
- When you encounter stressful situations during the day, ones that bring up responses of fear, anxiety, frustration or anger, bring to mind your focus word(s) and place your attention there. Over time, you will train your mind and body to respond to stresses with peacefulness instead of adrenaline.

On the next page, log your first several Relaxation Responses. Note how you felt before and after, the effect of your focus word(s) on your state of mind, any images that arose, the level and content of your intrusive thoughts, the ease or difficulty of passively disregarding them.

*Meditation available on audio tape.

🍃 Relaxation Response Log

Date _____

Date _____

Date _____

Date _____

Date _____

Section Four

What is Wellness?

What is Wellness?

Two of my greatest teachers about the true meaning of wellness are my friends Sarah Becker and Judith Mahrer, who both died of cancer in 1996.

Sarah

Sarah was 41 when she was diagnosed with pancreatic cancer in 1993. A beautiful, vibrant dance/movement therapist, she was the picture of health, and a wonderful role model for nutrition, exercise, and holistic lifestyle.

The doctors didn't give her a timeline for the progression of her disease, but we all knew it couldn't be good. Pancreatic cancer, from what we had heard and read, was one of the most virulent types, often carrying a life expectancy of only months from diagnosis.

But Sarah completely ignored the prevailing groupthink about pancreatic cancer, and focused instead on turning her incredible will and spirit toward beating what she called "this cancer thing." First, she claimed her place on her treatment team, notifying her doctors that she wanted to be educated and informed. She read stacks of papers, pamphlets, books and reports on everything from chemotherapy and radiation to acupuncture and affirmative prayer. In consultation with her doctors, she mapped out a strategy for herself that included assertive medical remedies, along with complementary resources such as massage, lymph drainage, nutrition, journal writing and Chinese herbology.

Next, Sarah gathered her community around her. She invited several friends for an elegant high tea at the Brown Palace Hotel. She reached out to family and friends from whom she had drifted apart. Her leadership roles in the local and national dance therapy associations continued.

Sarah always loved a hearty laugh, and she planned humor into her days. We often went to comedies in movie theaters, or rented them on video. As a former New Yorker, *Seinfeld* was her favorite television show. Her friends made her 6-hour tapes of *Seinfeld* episodes, and she laughed until she cried.

She joined support groups and extended her community to include others who were leaning into life-threatening illness. She began attending church. Sarah continued to spend time in nature, although her formerly vigorous hikes became strolls through parks and drives to the mountains. She continued to live alone, in a home she loved, clear and focused that she wanted to maintain her independence as long as she possibly could.

Finally, nearly three years after diagnosis, Sarah agreed to enter hospice. I'll never forget the party she convened the night before she was transferred. Her living room and kitchen were filled with balloons, flowers, her favorite foods (which she couldn't

From Kay's Journal, February 1996

*Spent yesterday at hospice with Sarah.
When I got there, she was sitting in a chair,
taking up all the space, looking so much like her
old self that I was actually startled. She sat in
her chair like a queen, regal, imperious.
I asked if she wanted to go outside for a little
walk. Her mom and I bundled her up in
ski parka, hat, scarf, gloves, pillows, afghans,
blankets. We took her in a wheelchair into
the balmy 65-degree day, spring-like, bright blue
skies, thin sunshine, robins chirping, thick yellow
cats rubbing up against her bundled feet. Each
moment was the last moment. This is the last cat.
The last tree. The last sunshine on face. The last
bright blue sky. The sidewalk cracks were painful
to her so we made a labyrinth, weaving the
wheelchair around the bumpy parts.
Sarah's last dance.*

eat, but wanted us to), her family and friends. Her strength was all but gone, her energy sapped, but her vitality remained.

Sarah spent about two weeks in hospice. A few days before she died, I wrote the journal entry on the opposite page.

She died peacefully early one morning, cocooned in a circle of love, with her mother holding one hand and her best friend the other.

Judith

Judith was a self-described "late bloomer," a woman who began coming into her own in her 50s. She was an amazing weaver of people, with networking capabilities that reached cross-culturally and around the globe. Possessed of a brilliant mind and an innate resonance to beauty in all forms, she was a poet, writer, dreamer, visionary and journeyer.

Judith was also possessed of a melancholy, a deep regret for what she feared were her "wasted years" of missed connections, opportunities and dreams. She struggled with the seeming paradox that she was so gifted at negotiating opportunities and connections for others, but had difficulty believing in herself and trusting her own judgment and choices.

Her cancer was extremely sudden in onset and decline. One day, just before her 62nd birthday, she went to the doctor for problems that had concerned but not alarmed her. The next week she was admitted to hospice. I was out of town during the transition, so I was shocked and dismayed to hear the news, and rushed to her bedside as soon as I could.

The change in Judith was palpable from the moment I entered the room. She was clear, focused, in charge and in control. Any shred of hesitation or indecision was gone. She knew what she wanted, whether it was a backrub, a pain pill, a pretty scarf to dress up her hospital gown, or a meditation read aloud to her. She spoke from a place of deep knowing about the Mystery of death. She told me about forgiveness and release and the intimacy of Spirit. The fears and insecurities that had haunted her were replaced with luminous poise and intense curiosity. During one of our last visits she peered at me through vibrant eyes and said, "You know, Kay, I think dying is just about the most interesting thing I've ever done."

During our last visit together, I read the poetry she loved so much — Rumi, Robert Bly, William Carlos Williams, Mary Oliver, Emily Dickenson, David Whyte. After some hesitation, I read Mary Oliver's poem, "When Death Comes." She sighed as I read the lines,

> *When it's over, I want to say: All my life*
> *I was a bride married to amazement,*
> *I was the bridegroom, taking the world into my arms.*

I will dance...

Journal entry by Judith K. Mahrer
Written in writing group as her 60th birthday present to herself

I will dance in the meadow with sunbeams reflecting off the pond. I will eat moonbeam ice cream. I will wear beautiful, multi-colored garments woven from specially dyed yarns. I will sing magical songs to my grandchildren which they will remember all their lives and sing to their children. I will correspond with mythic heroes and heroines, long dead, who will share their secrets with me. I will incorporate their stories into my own writing.

I will travel on magic carpets to far-away lands and meet people whose language I miraculously understand and whose food I will find delicious. I will become a wise woman whose experiences everyone will learn from. I will achieve immortality before I die. I will be outrageous, dancing in the meadow of my life, wrapped in moonbeams, decorated with stars and singing ancient songs with words I never knew before. I will grow into myself, I will become who I truly am. I will write all this down to share with others. I will keep my promises to myself.

Judith did, indeed, achieve a certain immortality before she died. In our last visit, I told her I was going to begin the Judith K. Mahrer Scholarship Fund through the National Association for Poetry Therapy Foundation. She died knowing that her name would stand for continuing education in the field she loved.

And when the poem was over, and the last syllables had dissolved like musical notes into the air, she opened her eyes, smiled at me, squeezed my hand weakly, and said, "I am a bride, married to amazement."

Judith died two days later, peaceful and brave. And, I imagine, amazed.

When Death Comes

What is your reaction to the stories of Sarah and Judith? Is there one you identify with more?

How close have you personally come to death? Tell about your experience.

Have you ever been with someone as they died? What was that like for you?

What are your feelings about death? About your own death?

Do you believe in an afterlife? What do you think happens to people/souls when they die?

What do you think will happen to you/your soul when you die? Does this thought comfort you?

If you were told that your death could be reasonably predicted in a finite number of years or months, how might you (or did you) react? What might you do (or are you doing) in your remaining time?

If you were told that your death could be reasonably predicted but that your life could be significantly extended if you changed some of your habits and behaviors, what would (or did) you think about changing? Would you be (are you) willing to change? Would you be (are you) able to change?

There are some essential qualities of wellness that we might discern from the stories of Sarah and Judith. These foundational principles and concepts guide the processes in this workbook.

🍃 The Essential Qualities of Wellness

1. **Wellness is a state of mind.** It does not necessarily require physical vigor and vitality. It is an attitude, a worldview, a philosophy of life.

What is your attitude or philosophy about wellness?

2. **Healing is not the same as curing.** Judith and Sarah's cancers were incurable, but that did not stop them from healing themselves at mental, emotional and spiritual levels. Healing, as used in this context, refers to the proactive thoughts, actions, attitudes and beliefs that come *from the inside out* to effect a positive difference in body, mind, heart and spirit.

How do you define healing? How do you define curing?

3. **Wellness happens in the present tense.** Judith's shift to wellness happened almost instantaneously. Her present and future ceased to be determined by her past. She lived each moment as it was presented to her, and she did so from a mindset of wellness and healing.

How much of your time do you spend living in the past? How much in the future? How much in the present?

4. **Wellness requires self-determination.** As Sarah knew, it is essential to take your place as partner in the wellness team. Wellness is an active choice. No one can do it for you.

How do you empower yourself? Do you feel you are effective as a partner in your wellness team? Explore this.

5. **Wellness requires balance.** The circle of life requires that attention be paid to all aspects and elements of balanced living. This includes balancing work and recreation, time spent with others and with yourself, eating balanced meals, and making sure that your body/mind/heart/spirit are all receiving quality attention. During the three years of her illness, Sarah was a masterful role model of balance.

Where are you balanced? Where are you out of balance?

6. **Wellness requires peacemaking.** Wellness cannot thrive in an atmosphere of blame, resentment, negativity or doubt. Judith was a powerful teacher about making peace with yourself and others. Whatever it is that holds you back from peace, let it go. If it comes back, let it go again. Forgive yourself. Forgive others. Do this often.

Who or what in your life would benefit from forgiveness?

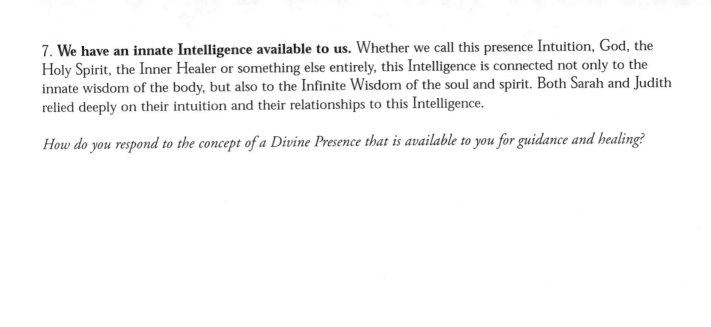

7. **We have an innate Intelligence available to us.** Whether we call this presence Intuition, God, the Holy Spirit, the Inner Healer or something else entirely, this Intelligence is connected not only to the innate wisdom of the body, but also to the Infinite Wisdom of the soul and spirit. Both Sarah and Judith relied deeply on their intuition and their relationships to this Intelligence.

How do you respond to the concept of a Divine Presence that is available to you for guidance and healing?

8. **Expression builds a bridge to wellness.** Expression and exploration of our thoughts and feelings help us bridge into wellness. Writing brings self-knowledge, self-awareness, release of limiting beliefs, transformation of old stories and celebration of new possibilities. Sarah and Judith were both avid journal writers. They continued writing and expressing as long as they were able, and left behind volumes of journals as testaments to their lives.

What is it within you that wants expression?

Reflect some more on these essential qualities of wellness. At first glance, some of this may seem repetitive. There are good reasons to complete these Sentence Stems anyway. One is that reframing these questions as statements is likely to elicit response from a different part of your awareness. Another is that repetition lets you layer down into even more of your true thoughts and feelings.

So give it a try. It should take about two or three minutes per Sentence Stem. But if you want more space or time, continue in the white space on this page.

🍃 Wellness Self-Assessment

Today's date _____

To me, wellness is........

Currently, my wellness state of mind is.......

The way that I differentiate between healing and curing is.......

My ability to live in the present is.......

The level of my self-determination about my health and wellness is......

The areas of my life where I feel balanced are.......

The areas of my life where I feel out of balance are......

When I think about making peace with myself and others, I realize.....

The innate Intelligence within me........

I build bridges to wellness by......

Someone who is a good role model of wellness for me is.......

As I review my responses to these Sentence Stems, I notice or am surprised by......

The Structured Write is an excellent technique to use any time you've surfaced something that is potentially difficult or anxiety-producing. Its structure gives you a comprehensive overview of an issue, while containing it in manageable pieces.

It's also very good when you want to get a quick once-over of clarity about a situation or question.

Choose something about your current reality that you'd like to explore. This could be a current illness, a chronic condition, an emotion, a challenging relationship, something that has surfaced from your "current reality" writes — anything at all!

Begin by completing the sentence, "I want to explore....."
with whatever topic you've chosen.
Then write one or two sentences for each prompt.
The entire process will take about 15 minutes.

🍃 Structured Write on Wellness

Today's date _____

The topic I want to explore is.......

The first thing that comes to mind.....

Beneath the surface I find......

I am disturbed or uncomfortable with......

I feel hopeful about.....

I would benefit from....

My next step is ....

Section Five

You and Your Healthy Self

A Character Sketch is a portrait of yourself, or some aspect of yourself. Sometimes it is easier to write an accurate Character Sketch if you observe yourself from the third person, as if you were writing about someone else. In this exercise, we'll write a Character Sketch of yourself during a typical day. During this process, please remember the key words *curious* and *compassionate*. The point isn't to notice all the things you're doing wrong or could be doing better. The point is simply to notice.

Read through the meditation on the next page. When you feel ready, begin to write. Keep writing for about 10 minutes.

*Meditation available on audio tape.

A Typical Day

Close your eyes and take a few deep breaths. On the exhales, focus on becoming comfortable in your body. Relax and release.

In this imagery, we're going to follow you through a typical day in your life. Begin with the moment you open your eyes.

How do you awaken? What was the quality of your sleep? What is the first sound you hear? What are the sights that greet you as you open your eyes? What are your first thoughts?

How do you arise? What are the everyday rituals that you perform at the first of the day? Check in with your emotions. How do you feel at the beginning of this new day?

Notice your activities, actions and thoughts as you proceed through the early hours. Where do you place your time and attention? What is your pace? Are there others whose needs must also be met? Look around at your home environment. What is the quality of your space? Notice the tone of your day so far.

And now move ahead to the time when you begin your day's activities. Notice whether you have a plan or schedule or if your time is open and fluid. Notice if there are distractions or interruptions..... stressful encounters..... and if so, how you handle them.

Notice how you care for yourself during the day..... what your meals are like..... the quality of your interactions with others...... the attention you offer to your body..... whether you move or stretch during the day. Remember to observe yourself with curiosity and compassion. There is no need for judgment or criticism.

As the sun begins to fall into the western sky, notice how you make the shift toward evening. What plans you have for your dinner hour and evening time. Notice how and with whom you spend your time and attention. Check in with your feelings. What has been accomplished today? What has been left undone? What is the level of your satisfaction?

And finally, turn your attention to how you close the day, how you prepare yourself for rest. What are your thoughts and feelings as you tuck yourself into bed? How has this day been for you physically? emotionally? mentally? spiritually?

Who or what is the last thing you interact with as you close your eyes? How would you rate your quality of life during this day? Just notice what you notice, and accept what comes. And when you are ready, turn to the next page and write about your typical day.

Write your Character Sketch of yourself during a typical day here. Try writing in the third person, as if you were a novelist describing the typical day of your main character.

When you're finished, re-read what you've written about A Typical Day, and give yourself some feedback. Use the white space below. What do you notice about the overall tone and quality of a typical day for you? What is your general level of satisfaction? Were there any surprises? Are there things you feel drawn to change about how you spend your days?

As I read this, I notice that....
.....I am surprised by.....
....I am curious about....
....I am aware of.....
...I feel....

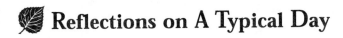 # Reflections on A Typical Day

Today's Date _____   Start Time _____   End Time _____

Now let's take a look at your Healthy Self.... the person you are becoming as you develop the qualities of wellness in your life. Again, you'll write a Character Sketch, but this time, let's write it in the first person — the "I/me/my" voice. Again, you'll write for about 10 minutes.

Read through this entrance meditation at least twice.* Again, if it's helpful, try some pleasant instrumental music in the background. Allow yourself to accept whatever images come, without spending too much time on what meaning they might have. We'll begin to deconstruct the meaning later on.

*Meditation available on audio tape.

Your Healthy Self

Find a comfortable position and begin to relax.
Take a deep breath.... and release it.
And take another deep breath.... and release it.

In your mind's eye, begin to create an image of yourself at a higher level of wellness. Regardless of your present state of physical health or wellness, imagine that you have attained a higher overall quality of life. How do you see yourself?

Let's take a closer look.

How do you see yourself physically? Are there changes to your physical appearance as you look at your Healthy Self? What do you notice about your posture, your clothing, the way you hold yourself? Check inside, and notice how you feel physically. Notice where you are relaxed and open. What is the quality of your well-being?

And now turn your attention to your mental state. What do you think about? What ideas are in your mind? What is the quality of your thoughts? Notice what fills your mind.

Next, begin to notice your emotions. Name and describe the feelings that you experience as your Healthy Self. Notice the quality of your emotions. Where do you experience them in your body? How do these emotions prepare you to deal with conflict or struggle? Take a few moments to connect with your emotional body.

And now turn your attention to your spiritual Healthy Self. What is the quality of your experience of Spirit.... God.... Jesus Christ.... Higher Power.... or whatever name you call the Divine. How does your Healthy Self connect with the Presence? What are the names of the qualities that fill the heart and soul of your Healthy Self? Qualities like peace of mind.... forgiveness.... gratitude..... love.....

Spend a few moments reflecting on the experience of your Healthy Self.

And when you are ready, turn the page and begin to write.

Write your Character Sketch of your Healthy Self here. Try writing in the first person and in the present tense, as if you describing yourself as you are, right now.

Again, re-read what you've written about your Healthy Self, and give yourself some feedback below. What do you notice about the overall tone and quality of your writing? Does this feel possible or attainable? Were there any surprises? What would it take to incorporate some of these qualities?

As I read this, I notice that....
.....I am surprised by.....
....I am curious about....
....I am aware of.....
...I feel....

Reflections on My Healthy Self

Today's Date _____   Start Time _____   End Time _____

Let's write a third Character Sketch. This time, we'll revisit the first meditation, but through the eyes and in the voice of your Healthy Self.* When you're ready, write for about 10 minutes.

*Meditation available on audio tape.

A Typical Day as Your Healthy Self

Close your eyes and take a few deep breaths. On the exhales, focus on becoming comfortable in your body. Relax and release.

In this imagery, we're going to follow your Healthy Self through a typical day. We'll refer to your Healthy Self as "you." So first bring to mind the image of your Healthy Self. Take a moment to imagine yourself stepping into the person you are becoming.

Now, begin with the moment you open your eyes.

How do you awaken? What was the quality of your sleep? What is the first sound you hear? What are the sights that greet you as you open your eyes? What are your first thoughts?

How do you arise? What are the everyday rituals that you perform at the first of the day? Check in with your emotions. How do you feel at the beginning of this new day?

Notice your activities, actions and thoughts as you proceed through the early hours. Where do you place your time and attention? What is your pace? Are there others whose needs must also be met? Look around at your home environment. What is the quality of your space? Notice the tone of your day so far.

And now move ahead to the time when you begin your day's activities. Notice whether you have a plan or schedule, or if your time is open and fluid. Notice if there are distractions or interruptions..... stressful encounters..... and if so, how you handle them.

Notice how you care for yourself during the day..... what your meals are like..... the quality of your interactions with others...... the attention you offer to your body..... whether you move or stretch during the day.

As the sun begins to fall into the western sky, notice how you make the shift toward evening. What plans do you have for your dinner hour and evening time? Notice how and with whom you spend your time and attention. Check in with your feelings. What has been accomplished today? What has been left undone? What is the level of your satisfaction?

And finally, turn your attention to how you close the day, how you prepare yourself for rest. What are your thoughts and feelings as you tuck yourself into bed? How has this day been for you physically? emotionally? mentally? spiritually?

Who or what is the last thing you interact with as you close your eyes? How would you rate your quality of life during this day? Just notice what you notice, and accept what comes. And when you are ready, turn to the next page and write about your typical day as your Healthy Self.

Write your Character Sketch of your Healthy Self during a typical day here. Again write in the first person "I" voice, in the present tense, as if this were the day you are experiencing right here, right now, today.

Re-read what you've written about A Typical Day as your Healthy Self, and give yourself some feedback. What do you notice about the overall tone and quality of a typical day for you? What is your general level of satisfaction? What feels easier, more spacious? Were there any surprises?

> *As I read this, I notice that....*
> *.....I am surprised by.....*
> *....I am curious about....*
> *....I am aware of.....*
> *...I feel....*

Reflections on A Typical Day as My Healthy Self

Today's Date _____ Start Time _____ End Time _____

Now we know where you are, and where you want to be. Let's build a bridge to your Healthy Self. Compare your first and third writes. Notice the similarities and differences between them. Now see if you can list at least ten actions you can take or continue that will help you bridge into your Healthy Self. If there are major life changes on your list, see if you can break them down into manageable steps. These examples are generic, but be as specific as you can.

Examples:

🍃 *Eat breakfast every day*

🍃 *Begin attending church or synagogue more regularly*

🍃 *Forgive someone who has hurt me*

🍃 *Lose weight using a healthy, realistic program of nutrition and exercise*

🍃 *Clean up the clutter in my house*

🍃 *Stop falling asleep to late-night television*

🍃 *Reduce the amount of time I spend in mindless activities*

🍃 *Start listening more and arguing less with my family*

🍃 *Set aside time every day for meditation or prayer*

🍂 Bridging Into Your Healthy Self

1.

2.

3.

4.

5.

6.

7.

8.

9.

10.

11.

12.

Now, assign each of these a ranking of 1 (hard!) to 10 (easy!), based on how easy it would be for you to actually begin making these changes, and how willing you are to actually do it. Circle or star the numbers of three to six changes you *could* and *would* do.

Select up to six behavioral changes you'd like to track that will move you in the direction of your Healthy Self. Get a package of self-adhesive foil stars, or use a felt-tipped pen. Tape this chart to your refrigerator or mirror; the visual reinforcement is an important factor in maintaining motivation and interest. Give yourself a star for each behavior you complete. You'll find a blank to photocopy in the Resources section at the end of this workbook.

Star Chart

for the week of _____

It takes 42 days to change a habit!

Task	Monday Date:	Tuesday Date:	Wednesday Date:	Thursday Date:	Friday Date:	Saturday Date:	Sunday Date:
How many times this week? _____							
How many times this week? _____							
How many times this week? _____							
How many times this week? _____							
How many times this week? _____							
How many times this week? _____							

from *The Write Way to Wellness: A Workbook for Healing and Change*, ©2000 Kathleen Adams, The Center for Journal Therapy. Permission is granted to reproduce for personal or educational use.

Section Six

The Healer Within

For this process,*
you will need colored pencils,
felt-tip markers or crayons.

Close your eyes and ask for an image of your Inner Healer....
the part of you that intimately knows the wisdom of your body,
that is connected to a wise and benevolent Intelligence,
that can be your guide, champion and protector
on this journey to wellness.

This image may come as a human,
or as any other sort of being — fish, fowl, four-legged, crawler —
or as an element of nature or the natural world,
or as a shape or color.

Close your eyes and ask that the Healer Within
reveal itself to you, in visual form.

When you have received an image of your Inner Healer,
stay there a few moments to fully absorb the details
and the feeling of the Healer Within.

Then, draw or sketch
a picture of it on the next page.

(Don't worry if you're not an artist.)

*Meditation available on audio tape.

A Picture of My Inner Healer

Today's Date _____   Start Time _____   End Time _____

On the next page,
write about your drawing.
(If you didn't draw, then close your eyes
and imagine your Inner Healer,
and then write about what your imagery.)

What do you notice?
What surprises you?
What are you aware of?
Reflect on the Healer Within.

🍃 Reflections on My Inner Healer

Today's Date _____ Start Time _____ End Time _____

The Healer Within

Today, this day, I
Heal myself. Today, this day, and
Every day, I

Heal myself and
Effortlessly allow
All peace, all joy, all
Love to flow through my
Essence like a
River.

Witness this:
I heal myself
This day,
Heal myself
In peace, in joy, in love,
Now, today, this day.

My Inner Healer

Merlin, I shall call you
You magician of the healing arts

I never knew I had a magician inside me
Never knew I could heal myself with you
Never knew you are always there for me
Eternally, you never sleep or
Rest, you're always working

Healing me and helping me to
Eventually learn to heal myself
Always there for me, always present, a-
Live and alert and telling me that
Everything will be okay, you're on the job
Rejoice!

AlphaPoem: The Healer Within

Write a poem about The Healer Within in which each successive line begins with the next letter of the phrase.

T

H

E

H

E

A

L

E

R

W

I

T

H

I

N

AlphaPoems are one of the easiest and most enjoyable
ways to write poetry....
especially if you think you're not a poet!

They're also surprisingly "write on" in the truth they tell.
You can write AlphaPoems using any word or phrase,
or the entire alphabet, A to Z
(it's x-ceptable to cheat on x-tra hard letters!)
or even just a random assortment of letters.

Let's try another AlphaPoem. This time, use the entire alphabet.
Here's an AlphaPoem called "Advice From My Inner Healer" written by a man in
one of my groups. He actually took this advice, and reports he is slowing down,
enjoying his life more, and his high blood pressure is decreasing.

Advice from my Inner Healer. He says—
Beneath the surface of your
Calm, collected exterior live many
Different
Emotions.
Feel them all.
Generosity is
Healing. Give of yourself, your time and talents and your money.
Identify
Just what is bothering you. Write it down.
Kindness is healing. Spread it around.
Lay about and rest instead of always trying to
Muscle your way through "just one more thing."
Never, ever, ever go to bed angry with your wife or kids.
Orange juice and club soda makes a refreshing drink.
Play with grandkids in the park.
Quilts are good for wrapping in to
Read good books on a cold winter day.
Symptoms are trying to
Tell you something. Listen to them.
Use your common sense to
View yourself as how you really are:
Warts and all, you're still a pretty
Xceptional man.
You can do about anything you decide you want.
Zest agrees with you.

AlphaPoem – Title: _____

A

B

C

D

E

F

G

H

I

J

K

L

M

N

O

P

Q

R

S

T

U

V

W

X

Y

Z

We talked in the Getting Started section about the Dialogue technique, and how it is a way of giving voice to the wisdom inside yourself.

Let's dialogue with the Inner Healer.*

Dialogues often take some time, so plan on at least a 30-minute writing session.
The first page of your writing space has cues to help you get in the flow of Dialogue.
Ignore them if they get in your way. And just keep going if you're not finished at the end of the page. There are more blank pages for the continuation of your Dialogue.

Before you begin, you may want to review the guidelines for satisfying dialogue on the next page.

Close your eyes and let yourself relax. Take a few deep breaths. Exhale fully.

Imagine that you are in a beautiful place in nature. A place where you feel rested, revitalized and healed.

In the distance, coming toward you, you see a being that you recognize as your Inner Healer. Take a moment to appreciate the image of your Inner Healer, noticing as you do the details of how s/he/it expresses in form.

When the two of you are within greeting distance, say hello, and ask if you can talk. Then begin to walk or sit together. Know that this is a part of you that holds your truth, that wants you to be well, and that knows how to help you heal.

Begin to hold a conversation in your mind. You'll find that you can easily translate this conversation to the written form. Remember that either of you can ask any question and receive an honest answer, and that either can make any statement, knowing it will be heard without judgment or criticism.

When you feel ready, begin to write your Dialogue with the Inner Healer.

*Meditation available on audio tape.

Dialogue with the Inner Healer

Me: _____

_____

_____

_____

Inner Healer: _____

_____

_____

_____

_____

_____

Me: _____

_____

_____

_____

Inner Healer: _____

_____

_____

_____

_____

Me: _____

_____

_____

_____

Inner Healer: _____

_____

_____

_____

_____

Suggestions for Satisfying Dialogue

Give yourself plenty of time.
This is a journal technique that usually takes at least 20 or 30 minutes.

Make sure you're comfortable, and free from distractions.
Once you get started with a Dialogue, you'll not want to be interrupted.

Start with an entrance meditation.
Imagine yourselves together in a beautiful place in nature,
  or in another special place that is healing for you.

Let yourself feel temporarily uncomfortable.
It is perfectly natural to feel as if you making it up and even to feel silly
or awkward. This feeling goes away with practice.

Have fun. Expect the unexpected.
This is part of the delight of this technique.

Respect the silence.
Sometimes you'll come to a place of pause. Just wait.
Close your eyes and breathe. Relax.
Ask inside, "What else am I to know?"
Then write what comes.

Exit gracefully.
When you feel finished, ask, "Is there anything else?"
If not, then thank your Dialogue partner, and ask if you may speak again.

Trust the process.
You may get answers and insights that seem to come from nowhere.
You may not recognize your insights as your own. The Dialogue technique
is a way of translating the nonverbal wisdom of the body into language. This
may feel strange or unsettling.
Trust yourself. Trust your body. Trust the process. Trust.

Continue your Dialogue with your Inner Healer on this page.

Body-Centered Dialogue Partners

Dialogue with your body.
Thank your body for its wonderful, miraculous service. Ask how you might express your appreciation.

Dialogue with pain.
Ask what message it is trying to communicate to you.

Dialogue with a specific body part or organ, perhaps one that is giving you trouble.
Ask what it wants and needs from you.

Dialogue with an illness.
Ask how it is your teacher.

Dialogue with an addiction or behavior, such as smoking, or drinking too much, or overeating.
Ask how you can get this need met in a healthier way.

Dialogue with your Healthy Self.
Ask how your Healthier Self would handle problems or obstacles that confront or confound you.

Dialogue with Wellness.
Ask for specific action steps you can take to have more Wellness in your life.

Dialogue with your subpersonalities — Your Inner Child, Inner Critic, Perfectionist, Lost Self.
Ask them what they have to say. Tell them what you need them to hear.

Complete your Dialogue here.

Section Seven

The Circle of Life

A key quality of wellness is balance, which might be defined as "right relationship."
When you are optimally balanced in an area of life, it may not be ideal or perfect, but you are content with what life has offered you in this area, and you experience peace of mind and heart. You know you are doing the best you can to maintain or improve this area of your life.

On the other hand, if you are out of balance/right relationship in an area, it may evoke feelings such as motivation to change, concern, dissatisfaction, frustration, or even resentment, anger, fear or despair.

On the facing page is a Balance Wheel divided into eight wedges.
Assume that the center of the circle represents the complete absence of balance/right relationship in each wedge, and the outer rim represents complete balance or optimum right relationship.

Where would you place yourself in each area of life balance? Draw a line. You may want to use crayons, colored pencils or markers to color in the sections.

If the categories seem too broad for you, feel free to subdivide your wedges. For instance, you may passionately love your volunteer work, but find your day job insufferable. Or you may have a terrific marriage, but poor relationships with your parents and siblings. Adjust the Balance Wheel to fit your circumstances. Just remember to label any sections you subdivide.

Career/Work/Activity: Job satisfaction, career choice, interests, mental stimulation, volunteer activities.

Relationships/Love/Family: Friends, family (birth and present), primary partnership/marriage, children, any other relationships in which you give/receive, or struggle with, love.

Fun/Recreation. Social activities, sports, leisure activities, vacations, absorbing or pleasurable activities, hobbies, play time, community groups.

Emotional Health/Personal Growth. Self-development, self-awareness, inner work, counseling, recovery groups, support groups, workshops, seminars, self-help books, self-nurturing practices.

Health/Body. Present state of wellness, nutrition, weight, exercise, healthy habits, body image, self-care, adequate sleep, medication management, presence or absence of illness/disease.

Home/Environment. Your domicile (house, neighborhood, city, state/region), as well as how you live, e.g. is clutter driving you nuts, is your living space clean enough, etc.

Finances/Security. Income adequate for living expenses, savings, investments, retirement, emergency funds, insurance, adequate medical coverage.

Spirituality/Religion. Personal awareness of/relationship with the Holy (by whatever name), a place for worship, spiritual/religious practice, community, philosophy about death/afterlife.

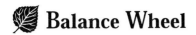

Balance Wheel

Today's Date _____   Start Time _____   End Time _____

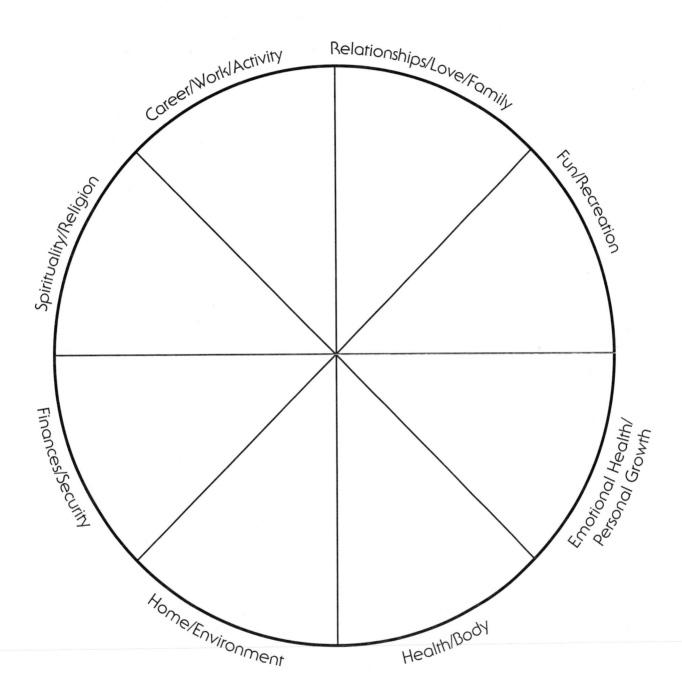

On the next page, jot some notes about the individual areas of the Balance Wheel. Which areas are out of balance? Are you aware of what would help you strengthen them? Which areas are well-balanced? To what do you attribute this balance?

![leaf] Reflections on the Balance Wheel

Today's Date _____   Start Time _____   End Time _____

Career/Work/Activity

Relationships/Love/Family

Fun/Recreation

Emotional Health/Personal Growth

Health/Body

Home/Environment

Finances/Security

Spirituality/Religion

Your individual prescription for wellness draws from your *core* or *primary* values — the qualities and characteristics that give your life meaning and purpose. On the next page you will find a long list of values. Circle the ones that resonate with you as essential to your life.

Your primary values will be the ones for which you can answer "yes" to this question:

> *Do I feel*
> > *dissatisfied*
> > *unfulfilled*
> > *deprived*
> > *unhappy*
> > *shut down*
> > *unlike myself*
> > *out of sorts*
> *if this quality or characteristic is "missing" in a situation,*
> *or if I am blocked from expressing it?*

🍂 Personal Values

Accomplishment	Fidelity	Prosperity
Achievement	Forgiveness	Providing for others/family
Acknowledgment	Forward-thinking	Psychic ability
Adventure	Freedom	Purity
Affection	Full Self-Expression	Religious beliefs
Appreciation	Generosity	Respect
Authenticity	Grace	Responsible citizenship
Balance	Gratitude	Risk-taking
Beauty	Harmony	Security
Benevolence	Healing ability	Self-actualization
Challenge	Health	Self-respect
Change and variety	Heart-centered	Serenity
Charisma	Helping others	Sexual attractiveness
Charity	Honesty	Sincerity
Clarity	Humor	Social activism
Cleanliness	Independence	Spiritual connection
Close relationships	Innovation	Status
Comfort	Integrity	Stewardship
Comfortable with death	Intimacy	Strength
Comfortable with self	Joy	Success
Communication	Leadership	Support
Community	Love	Surrender
Compassion	Mastery	Time for self
Consistency	Meaningful work	Time management
Courage	Mutuality	Togetherness
Creativity	Nature	Touch
Curiosity	Nonconformity	Trail-blazing
Decisiveness	Nurturing	Truth
Diversity	Organizational ability	Unconditional Love
Elegance	Passion	Vision
Empowerment	Patriotism	Vitality
Ethics	Peace of mind	Wealth
Excitement	Power	Wellness
Faith	Primary partnership	Wholeness
Fame	Privacy	Wisdom
Family	Progressive	World peace

We're now going to narrow your primary values down to ten core values. Go back to the prior page and consider the primary values you have circled. Notice if there are any that are naturally aligned, that might be combined or synthesized — *Honesty* and *Truth,* for instance, or *Family* and *Togetherness* and *Primary Partnership.*

Place a star by the values that seem vital and core to you. Test questions for this stage:

> *Has my alignment with this value been with me all my life?*
> *Have I always valued this quality or characteristic,*
> *even if I was blocked from expressing it?*

When you have your list down to ten, write them on the next page.

My Core Values

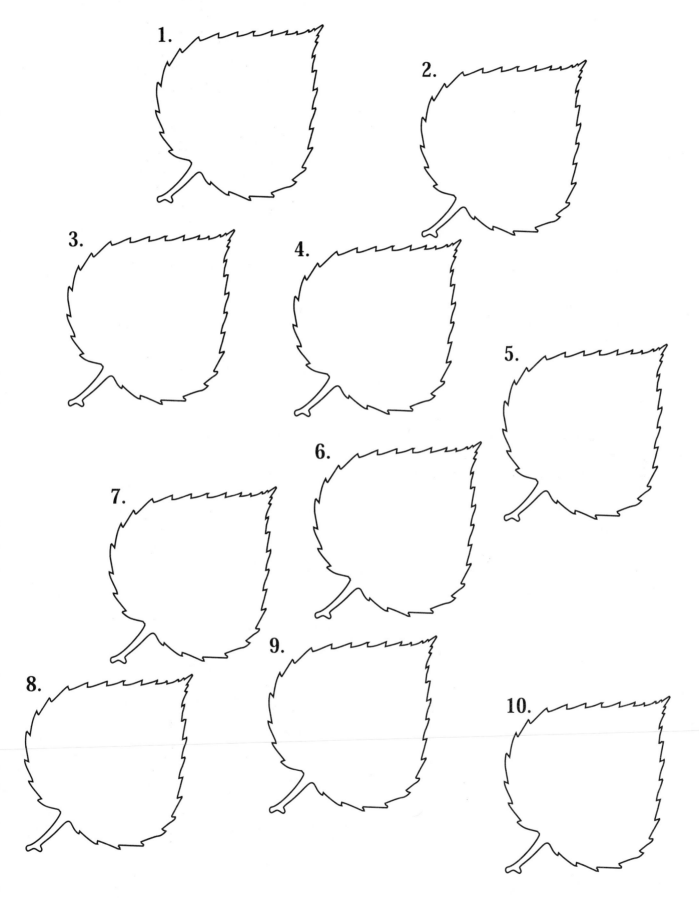

Now let's put your core values to work.

Bring to mind a situation that is troubling or difficult to you. It can be related to health, business, family, social relationships, success, anything at all. It can be a specific event, or a seemingly chronic condition.

Now scan over your list of core values and choose three of them. You might choose three that seem especially relevant to the situation, or you can choose three at random.

On the next page, first give a concise summary of the difficult situation. Then apply your first value to the situation. What might happen if you were to bring in this core value? What might shift, or how might you see the situation differently? What would the new possibilities be?

Repeat with the second value, and with the third. Use the white space on the back of the page if necessary.

There is a sample to review on the following page.

🍃 Applying Core Values

Today's Date _____ Start Time _____ End Time _____

A difficult or troublesome situation I am facing is

A brief synopsis of the situation is

If I applied my core value of _____ to this situation, then

If I applied my core value of _____ to this situation, then

If I applied my core value of _____ to this situation, then

🍃 Applying Core Values - Example

A difficult or troublesome situation I am facing is *I am scheduled to begin chemotherapy on Tuesday and I'm scared to pieces.*

A brief synopsis of the situation is *I had a malignant tumor removed five weeks ago and my doctor wants me to begin chemo. I trust my doctor and I believe she knows exactly what is right for me from a medical standpoint. But I'm scared and I don't want to do it, and I don't want anyone to know how scared I am.*

If I applied my core value of _____ humor _____ to this situation, then *I would be able to find something funny about it, I'm sure. I can watch videos like Patch Adams or read Erma Bombeck. I can watch carefully for the humor in this experience. So often something doesn't become funny until someone puts a humorous interpretation on it. I'm good at that. I can look for things that are humorous or ironic, and while I'm having the treatment I'll think about how I can make it a funny story to tell others when I'm home.*

If I applied my core value of _____ honesty _____ to this situation, then *I would be honest with my doctor and also with my family and let them know I'm scared and that I'm afraid I won't do well with chemo. I'm afraid of being weak and sick. I'm afraid of dying. I have been trying to be strong but I think that is not really very honest.*

If I applied my core value of _____ gratitude _____ to this situation, then *I would recognize how very grateful I am to be alive at all. My tumor was found in time and I gained unknown years of my life. I am so very grateful to God and to the doctors and my family and everyone who has stood by me through this. They will continue to stand by me and I will continue to be grateful and express my gratitude. Even when I am afraid I can still be grateful.*

Let's go back to the Balance Wheel again.

How might your core values support your efforts to seek and find more balance in your life?

Compare your list of ten core values to your Reflections on the Balance Wheel.

Notice especially the areas you wanted to bring into greater balance.

Which of your core values will most help you in this endeavor?

Bring to mind the image of your Inner Healer.

Request your Inner Healer to help you ask this test question:

What might the possibilities be if I brought more (value) to this area of my life?

Listen inside for the response of your Inner Healer.

The Healer Within may "speak" in nonverbal ways. You may receive images, flashes of insight, a "felt-sense" in the body, an "aha" of recognition, a subtle sense of "yes, this" or "no, not that."

When you identify core values that will help you achieve or maintain balance in each area of your life, jot the values in the wedges.

Then, on the back of the page or in the white space around the Balance Wheel, write your awarenesses:

If I applied my core value(s) of _____ to this situation, then.....

Applying Core Values to the Balance Wheel

Today's Date _____   Start Time _____   End Time _____

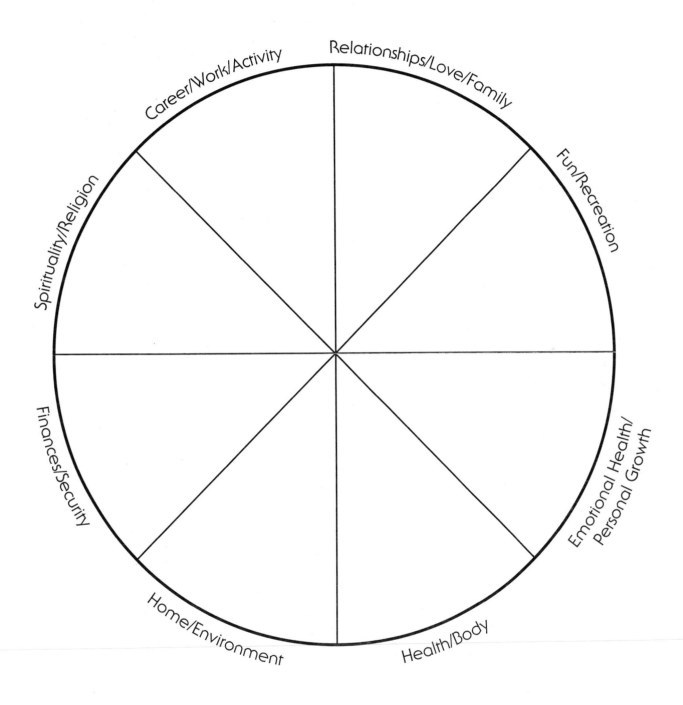

Section Eight

Managing Grief and Loss

On a dapple gray mare high atop the rolling hills outside of Guadalajara, I savored the dawn. Wisps of early morning mist wrapped the hillside in gauze as the emerging sun painted pastel brushstrokes against the clouds. Enrique, my guide, silently smoked a cigarette. The landscape brightened. I looked around, drinking in the beauty and the calm.

To the west, at the apex of a jutting cliff, three small white crosses caught the light. Using a combination of my best college Spanish and pantomime, I asked Enrique if we could go there for a closer look. He shook his head no.

My eyebrows made a question mark. *"Descansos,"* he said, flipping away the cigarette butt. He shrugged.

"¿Descansos?" I asked, searching for the word.

"Descansos," he agreed. He raised his hand to his throat and made an almost imperceptible sign of the cross.

Descansar. To rest. Ah. A resting place. These must be graves. We turned our horses the other way and headed into the sun.

Years later I discovered that *descansos* is a custom of erecting or painting a cross at the site where *muerte,* death, occurred. These crosses serve as markers for grieving and remembrance. Three people lost their lives on top of that cliff outside of Guadalajara, and the crosses bore witness to the fact.

Witnessing our losses. Placing small markers there. Healing from grief begins with remembrance.

On the next page, begin to name your losses. Let them come in any order, without regard for whether this "should" be an important loss. Next to your loss, write the year or your age when you experienced it.

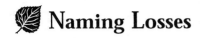

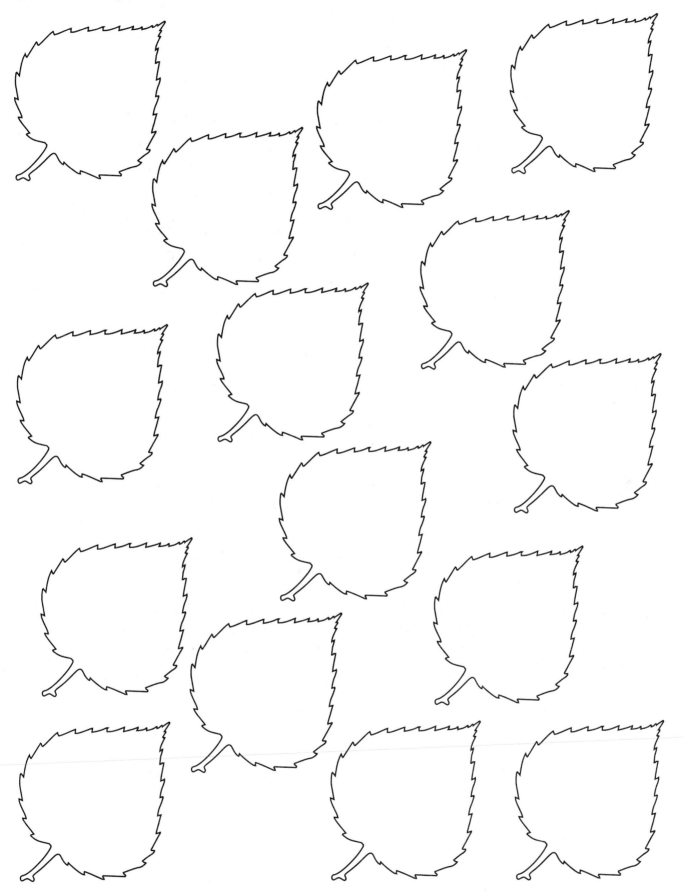

Grief is a natural response to the loss of something meaningful. This can be a person or relationship, a lifestyle, a dream or vision, a job, health, innocence, a pet, a deeply held belief or cherished ideal, or anything else that is emotionally valued.

In American culture, we tend to discount the validity of grief. We take an afternoon off for a funeral. If the death was in our immediate family, perhaps we take a long weekend before we're back at work. The old-fashioned custom of wearing black for a year to mark a natural cycle of loss and mourning seems charming but downright odd.

And we don't even talk about the *muertes pequeños* — the small losses that dot our everyday lives. The runner who pulls a ligament and cannot run. The promotion that went to a younger, less experienced, more aggressive co-worker. Putting the family pet to sleep. The inability to conceive a child. Thinning hair, or a thickening waistline. An auto accident that leaves a permanent decrease in range of motion. They happen every day. More often than not, we don't even mention them as losses, or acknowledge the depth of our sadness.

Grief is often cumulative. When something finally does trigger the grief response, we end up heartsick over not only the loss that has finally captured our attention, but all the losses that have been silently absorbed.

In the next two exercises, you will have the opportunity to first list your own *descansos* — a lifetime's worth of losses — and then to begin releasing your grief.

You'll find a Loss Lifeline on the next page. Starting with birth and proceeding by half-decade, mark your losses by naming them beneath the line. You may want to have crayons or colored pencils available to decorate your loss line. If you are age 70 or over, continue the lifeline in the white space on this page.

 **Loss Lifeline**

Birth   5   10

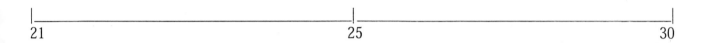

11   15   20

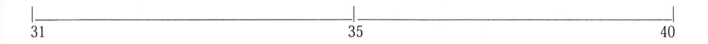

21   25   30

31   35   40

41   45   50

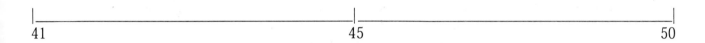

51   55   60

61   65   70

A Meditation on Grief*

This meditation is sourced in a Native American grieving ritual that a friend from the Souix Nation shared with me.

Close your eyes and take some deep breaths. Relax.

Place your hands on your belly. Allow yourself to breathe all the way down. Let your breath fill your belly. Follow the gentle rise and fall of your hands as you breathe.

Imagine now that you are walking alone in a quiet forest. Your only companion is your grief.

Walk deeply into the forest. Feel your grief walking with you, in your heart, in your belly.

Walk into the forest until you find a clearing, a place that feels right. A place to grieve.

The earth is soft beneath your feet. Kneel into the soft earth. Kneel, and place your hands palm-down on the Great Mother Earth.

With your heart and your belly full of grief, begin to dig into the earth with your hands. Begin to make a hollow. Dig a hole in the earth that is perhaps two feet in diameter, and two feet deep. Hold your grief in your awareness as you dig into the earth with your hands.

Allow yourself to feel your grief. Feel it fully, actively. Feel the anguish and the pain. Feel the sadness and the loss. Feel the anger. Feel the helplessness. Feel it all.

Name your griefs as you dig. Name them one by one. Call them out, into the earth, into the quiet forest, into the silent wind. Allow yourself to name your griefs and losses.

When your hole is dug, imagine that you place yourself face-down, with your belly and heart over the hollowed-out earth. Pour your grief into the earth. Make the sounds of mourning. Wail. Keen. Moan. Ohhhhh. Ahhhhh. Release yourself to the earth. That's right. Let it go. Trust that the earth is strong enough and compassionate enough to absorb and hold your pain.

Stay in the grieving place as long as you wish. When you are ready, imagine that you can arise from the earth, carefully fill in the hollow, leaving your grief with the Mother. Fill in the hollow and stamp it down. Stamp gently upon the earth, leaving your grief in her compassionate heart.

And when you are ready, begin to find your way out of the forest. Notice how you feel. Notice if your feelings have shifted from the time you entered the forest. Give thanks to Mother Earth for her strength and compassion. Give thanks to yourself for your willingness to grieve.

When you are ready, gently bring yourself back to normal awareness.

Write about your grieving meditation.

*Meditation available on audio tape.

122

🍂 Grieving Meditation

Today's Date _____   Start Time _____   End Time _____

_____

_____

_____

_____

_____

_____

_____

_____

_____

_____

_____

_____

_____

_____

_____

_____

_____

_____

_____

_____

_____

_____

_____

Journal Suggestions for Grief

When grief is new, feelings are so close to the surface and pain is so raw that short, structured techniques are most helpful.

Time feels like an enemy when you're adjusting to a loss, so it's comforting and reassuring to document your movement through it. You can do this by numbering the pages of your journal and only writing on one side of the page. Or try writing in a one-year diary with preprinted pages.

Because it is common for memory to be affected with acute grief, make to-do lists, and keep them right in your journal or day planner.

Write three words describing your feelings at the beginning and end of every journal entry. This helps you track your feelings over time and gives you an opportunity to notice that emotions shift with time and process.

Write Unsent Letters to and from, and Dialogues with, the sources of your mourning.

Captured Moments help you hold precious memories closely.

Write a "One Year from Today"* entry in which you fast-forward yourself to the healing side of the grief. Allow yourself a glimpse into the future. Imagine your life as if you have wheeled around through four seasons, and you are one year distant from the losses you are experiencing today.

*Meditation available on audio tape.

One Year From Today

Date: _____ (Today's Date, Next Year)

Section Nine

The Mystical Keys to Wellness

Love.
Gratitude.
Forgiveness.
Joy.
Grace (benevolence or blessing).

These five mystical keys to wellness enhance your state of mind and being, no matter what illness, disease, pain or suffering you may be experiencing. These five keys and their derivatives (peace of mind and heart, happiness, contentment, laughter) unlock the secrets to health, harmony and abundant living.

Let's begin our exploration with Sentence Stems. If you wish, you might use the white space on this page to Cluster one or more of the mystical keys before you complete the Sentence Stems.

Five Mystical Keys

Love

Love is......

I love.....

I am loved by.....

Gratitude

Gratitude is.....

I am grateful for....

Some "blessings in disguise" in my life are....

129

Forgiveness

Forgiveness is.....

Some people or circumstances I could forgive are....

I forgive myself for.....

Joy

Joy is.....

I feel joyful when.....

Some things that make me laugh.....

Grace

Grace is......

I experience the benevolence or blessing of grace when.....

I ask for a miracle of grace now for.....

Loving Kindness Meditation*

The Loving Kindness meditation is an ancient prayer from the Buddhist tradition. Say it many times to yourself. Make up a simple tune for it and chant it like a song.

> *May I be filled with loving kindness.*
> *May I be well.*
> *May I be peaceful and at ease.*
> *May I be happy.*

Begin with yourself. Send this loving kindness, this wellness, this peace and ease, this joy to yourself. See how difficult it is to hold a grudge or hang on to resentment when you are filling yourself with loving kindness. Notice how your heart opens and your soul stirs.

> *May you be filled with loving kindness.*
> *May you be well.*
> *May you be peaceful and at ease.*
> *May you be happy.*

Next, send this loving kindness to another. Begin with the ones you love most dearly. Bring these faces and beings into your meditation. Repeat this meditation silently, or out loud, or as a chant. Send loving kindness, wellness, peace, ease, joy to them. Notice how easy it is to wish these mystical keys of wellness for the ones you love.

Now web it out. Repeat the loving kindness meditation, holding in your awareness those you know and like. Friends, acquaintances, co-workers, neighbors. Notice how your heart expands as you expand the circle of loving kindness.

Next, send loving kindness to everyone you see and encounter but don't really know. The neighbors two streets over. The letter carrier. The cashier at the grocery store. Now, send it to those you don't like. Who are different from you. Whom you don't trust. Who are of the "wrong" political party, religion, ethnic background, national origin. Try sending loving kindness to terrorists and child molesters, rapists and drug dealers. To your enemies. The person who broke into your house and stole your stereo. The one who left you for another. The one you were left for. The bad driver who almost caused an accident. Your parents, for not giving you what you needed or wanted. Everyone you can think of who needs to be forgiven, for anything.

> *May we be filled with loving kindness.*
> *May we be well.*
> *May we be peaceful and at ease.*
> *May we be happy.*

Finally, close your meditation by creating a great big circle of loving kindness and including within it everyone you have brought to mind. Your dearest love and the most heinous criminal, your hairdresser and your best friend from grade school, the one who hurt you and the one you hurt. Include yourself. Send out loving kindness, wellness, peace, ease and joy.

Do this often.

*Meditation available on audio tape.

Reflections on Loving Kindness

Today's Date _____   Start Time _____   End Time _____

> *"I am a little pencil in the hand of a writing God*
> *who is sending a love letter to the world."*
>
> — Mother Teresa

Write a love letter.

To someone you love, or someone you used to love, or someone you want to love but your anger gets in the way. To yourself, or a part of yourself that yearns for redemption, or your body, or your illness — even if you hate your illness. *Especially* if you hate your illness.

To someone who hasn't yet been born, or someone who is no longer living. To someone you admire, or someone you've never met, or someone who is famous, or someone who has changed your life forever through a book or a prayer or a speech or a random comment on an airplane.

Let's assume for the time being that this letter will go no farther than here. You can write it as if it will not be read by the one you're writing to. So let yourself say whatever you want. Let yourself write freely. If you change your mind later and want to send it, that's up to you.

Begin with the phrase, *My heart wants to tell you......*

 **A Love Letter**

Today's Date _____   Start Time _____   End Time _____

Dear

My heart wants to tell you......

Love,

"If the only prayer we say in our lifetime is 'thank you,' that would suffice."

— Meister Ekhart

There's nothing like naming and claiming your gratitudes to help your blessings multiply and grow.

On the next pages, make a list of things you are grateful for.

See if you can get all the way to 100.

It's okay to repeat! Just write the next thing in your mind.

After you have named 100 things you are grateful for, you will understand why gratitude is a mystical key to wellness.

🍂 100 Gratitudes

Today's Date _____   Start Time _____   End Time _____

1 _____	26 _____
2 _____	27 _____
3 _____	28 _____
4 _____	29 _____
5 _____	30 _____
6 _____	31 _____
7 _____	32 _____
8 _____	33 _____
9 _____	34 _____
10 _____	35 _____
11 _____	36 _____
12 _____	37 _____
13 _____	38 _____
14 _____	39 _____
15 _____	40 _____
16 _____	41 _____
17 _____	42 _____
18 _____	43 _____
19 _____	44 _____
20 _____	45 _____
21 _____	46 _____
22 _____	47 _____
23 _____	48 _____
24 _____	49 _____
25 _____	50 _____

Brother David Stendl-Rast says that part of his spiritual practice is to find one new thing to be grateful for each day, something he has never praised before. Although he says he was worried at first that he might run out of new things to be grateful for, it hasn't happened yet.

Try looking for gratitude in unusual or hidden places.

Make a practice of writing a list of gratitudes every day. Your list may only have one item on it, or three, or five. Keep your list on your wall calendar, in your time management book, on your computer or in one of those small locking diaries that have one page for each day of the calendar year.

🍃 100 Gratitudes, continued

51 _____   76 _____

52 _____   77 _____

53 _____   78 _____

54 _____   79 _____

55 _____   80 _____

56 _____   81 _____

57 _____   82 _____

58 _____   83 _____

59 _____   84 _____

60 _____   85 _____

61 _____   86 _____

62 _____   87 _____

63 _____   88 _____

64 _____   89 _____

65 _____   90 _____

66 _____   91 _____

67 _____   92 _____

68 _____   93 _____

69 _____   94 _____

70 _____   95 _____

71 _____   96 _____

72 _____   97 _____

73 _____   98 _____

74 _____   99 _____

75 _____   100 _____

from *The Write Way to Wellness: A Workbook for Healing and Change,* ©2000 Kathleen Adams, The Center for Journal Therapy. Permission is granted to reproduce for personal or educational use.

For all the things I've said or done, not
Only recently but in the past
Readily acknowledging that they may have
Given hurt
I really never meant them in such a way so I
Very much am asking for forgiveness
Either for the person I am
Now or for the person I was then
Every day in every way,
Support me in forgiving myself, Oh Holy
Spirit, my mediator and forgiver.

Fill yourself with what you need, for
Only when you feel solid within can you
Really
Give. We are so
Intent upon blame and punishment, call it a
Victory to point at a mistake,
Even though this
Never solves the problem.
Enter into a
Space where you honor the One — Other or
Self — for gnawing unmet need or
   misdirected good intention.

*Thanks to the Monday afternoon writing group
for permission to use their Forgiveness poems,
written on Rosh Hashana 1999.*

From an inner place
Of sadness, grieving,
Regretting what might have been,
Going for the guts of
It all, the
Very quintessence of the loss,
   I grope for answers in
Every passing book, thought, speech to
kNow the primal grief, the primal sin of
Eve as she searched for knowledge
   and accepted the gift of the
Serpent — an easy way — and yet what
   was available to her, and
So I forgive her

Flowing outward, like the sea. Loose and
Open, spacious, porous,
Rhythmic, wise, Divinely
Guided to your new
Internal home. Let the
Very right next thing
Emerge. There is no
Need for struggle or regret.
Even now the
Silence speaks:
Surround yourself in peace.

For give is part
Of the word.... which means
Rightly or wrongly
Giving yourself something, giving
In to letting go of holding on.
View it differently. Give yourself something
Entirely, eternally, exquisitely yours.
Nothing is a greater challenge, sacrifice
   or freedom.
Expressing forgiveness brings peace,
Satisfies the voices,
Salves the soul.

![leaf] AlphaPoem: Forgiveness

Today's Date _____   Start Time _____   End Time _____

F

O

R

G

I

V

E

N

E

S

S

Meditation on Forgiveness*

Close your eyes and take some deep breaths. All the way down.
Release fully on the exhale.
Allow yourself to relax. There is nothing else for you to do. Nowhere else for you to be.
That's right. Just breathe, and relax, and be still.

We are going to take a journey of forgiveness.
Imagine yourself in a beautiful place in nature. See yourself there.
Smell the scented air, feel the breeze on your cheek, hear the murmurs and sounds around you.
Look around. See the generosity of nature. Appreciate the gifts. Notice how nature forgives:
A deadened tree becomes a home for insects. A forest fire becomes the catalyst for new growth.
A rainbow blossoms after every storm.
Now bring into the scene the image of your Inner Healer.
Welcome this Presence. Be still together.

Through the magic of imagery, you will find that you and your Inner Healer
can communicate without words. Your every image and thought is translated for you.
Your Inner Healer will help you with forgiveness.

Bring to mind a situation in your life that would benefit from healing.
A misspoken word, a broken trust, an unholy deed.
Perhaps you were wronged. Perhaps you wronged someone.
Bring the situation to mind, and give it to your Inner Healer.
Ask sincerely for forgiveness. Then turn it over.

Repeat the loving kindness meditation as you do.
May I be filled with loving kindness. May I be well.
May I be peaceful and at ease. May I be happy.
May you be filled with loving kindness. May you be well.
May you be peaceful and at ease. May you be happy.
May we be filled with loving kindness. May we be well.
May we be peaceful and at ease. May we be happy.

May all beings be peaceful. May all beings be free. May all beings be forgiven.

Let your Inner Healer do the work of forgiveness. Trust that the Healer Within knows how.
When you are ready, gently bring yourself back to normal awareness.
Write about your forgiveness meditation.

*Meditation available on audio tape.

Forgiveness Meditation

Today's Date _____   Start Time _____   End Time _____

"The practice of forgiveness is our most important contribution to the healing of the world."

— Marianne Williamson

Captured Moments* are short vignettes that freeze a moment of time permanently in prose, just as a camera shutter captures a moment of time on film.

They are characterized by their intensity of description. This is a place to allow yourself to use all the luscious, rich, evocative images, adjectives, verbs that you can find.

For this writing process, close your eyes and recall moments of joy.
Moments of pure, unadulterated bliss.

The birth of a child. A glorious sunset. The first time you skied moguls.
Swimming with dolphins. Ecstatic prayer. The finish line of a marathon.
Sailing on the lake. The view from the summit. Your photo in the newspaper.

Remember them all. Parade them before you. Re-enter the joy. Remember the thrill.

Choose one, and write about it on the next page. Be flowery. Be intense. Be dramatic!

"Always remember, joy is not incidental to your spiritual quest. It is vital."

— Hasidic teacher Rebbe Nachman of Buslov

*Meditation available on audio tape.

🍂 Captured Moment of Joy

Today's Date _____   Start Time _____   End Time _____

*"The winds of grace are always blowing,
but you have to raise the sail."*

— Ramakrishna

Grace.
Ineffable, unearned, benevolent.
The generosity of Spirit, inserted unmistakably in human life.
Protection. Preservation. An accident averted, a split-second intuition,
a miraculous recovery, remission.
Grace.
A glimpse into the Mysteries. A pulling back of the veil,
a momentary permeability between this world and the next.

Write a story about a time you experienced Grace.*

*Meditation available on audio tape.

A Time of Grace

Today's Date _____   Start Time _____   End Time _____

We have come to the end of this journey together. I leave you now to travel with your Inner Healer, your Healthy Self, your Core Values, your Mystical Keys.... and your journal.

Remember, everything you have learned in this workbook can be applied to a spiral notebook, three-ring binder or blank bound book. You have not only had experiences. You have also learned tools and techniques that will guide you for a lifetime.

And just in case you desire more structure, many of the forms and worksheets are found in the next section. They are left blank for you to copy and use as many times as you wish.

It is time to say goodbye to this phase of your journey. Take a few moments to page through this book. Review for yourself what all you have achieved and learned. Then, one last time, reflect and synthesize your findings.

Peace be with you.

May you be filled with loving kindness.

May you be well.

🍂 What I Have Learned

Today's Date _____   Start Time _____   End Time _____

Additional Resources

Good Books on Writing and Wellness

Writing

Adams, Kathleen. **Journal to the Self: 22 Paths to Personal Growth.** 1990, Warner Books. A comprehensive book featuring a technique approach to journal writing with emphasis on the therapeutic and healing aspects of reflective writing. Also: **The Way of the Journal: A Journal Therapy Workbook for Healing,** 2nd Ed., 1998, Sidran Press. A self-paced workbook featuring an approach that helps structure and contain writing without imposing limitations. Especially helpful for those who have had difficulty starting or staying with a journal program and those in psychotherapy or counseling programs.

Baldwin, Christina. **Life's Companion: Journal Writing as Spiritual Quest.** 1990, Bantam Books. The author offers many writing exercises to open the writer to higher consciousness, linking spiritual experiences with inner development and increased capacity for wellness.

Bouton, Eldonna. **Loose Ends.** 1999, Whole Heart Publications. A journal workbook for completing unfinished business through letter-writing. Over 30 simple and direct prompts, with space to write on the facing page.

Capacchione, Lucia. **The Well-Being Journal** and others. Combines non-dominant-hand drawing and dialogue to give voice to the Inner Healer and the body. Also: **The Power of Your Other Hand,** a theoretical treatment of non-dominant-hand writing and drawing.

DeSalvo, Louise. **Writing as a Way of Healing.** 1999, HarperSanFrancisco. How to use the Pennebaker studies to support physical and emotional healing. Includes excerpts and stories of the healing journeys of many well-known writers.

Fox, John. **Poetic Medicine.** 1997, Tarcher/Putnam. A gold mine of activities and ways of thinking about poetry as healer. Also: **Finding What You Didn't Lose.** 1995, Tarcher/Putnam.

Holzer, Burghild Nina. **A Walk Between Heaven and Earth.** 1994, Bell Tower. An exquisite exploration of journal writing as a meditation and creative process.

Metzger, Deena. **Writing for Your Life.** 1992, HarperSanFrancisco. A thorough exploration of the nature of creativity and the healing which comes from the creation and writing of your story, both personal and mythic.

Pennebaker, James W. **Opening Up: The Healing Power of Expressing Emotions.** 1997, Guilford Press. The research psychologist who first studied the impact of cathartic writing on healing gives a behind-the-scenes glimpse into how writing heals. Very interesting and readable.

Rainer, Tristine. **The New Diary.** 1978, Tarcher. One of the original three journal writing books, it remains an excellent resource on how journal writing heals. Clear and well-written. Also: **Your Life as Story: Writing the New Autobiography.** 1997, Tarcher. An excellent guide to a serious treatment of life story and autobiography.

Wellness

Anderson, Greg. **The 22 Non-Negotiable Laws of Wellness.** 1995, HarperCollins. In 1984, the author was given a cancer prognosis with 30 days to live. He began actively applying these laws of wellness, brought himself back from the brink of death, and dedicated himself to sharing the laws.

Benson, Herbert. **The Relaxation Response.** 1976, Avon Books. The simple meditative technique that has helped millions cope with fatigue, anxiety and stress. Also: **Timeless Healing.** 1996, Fireside. Practical help in conquering and preventing illness based on tangible proof that belief can heal.

Borysenko, Joan. **Minding the Body, Mending the Mind.** 1988, Bantam. A classic in the mind/body medicine field, from a pioneer in psychoneuroimmunology.

Caudill, Margaret A. **Managing Pain Before It Manages You.** 1995, Guilford Press. A practical, prescriptive workbook for pain management.

Davis, Martha, et. al. **The Relaxation and Stress Reduction Workbook, 4th Ed.** An excellent resource for putting together your own stress management program.

Dossey, Larry. **Reinventing Medicine.** 1999, HarperCollins. A compelling vision of the future of health and healing that incorporates the power of spiritual practices.

Ivker, Robert. **The Complete Self-Care Guide to Holistic Medicine.** 1999, J.P. Tarcher. A very helpful guide that presents alternative and mainstream treatments side-by-side.

Levine, Stephen. **A Year to Live.** 1997, Bell Tower. How to live each moment mindfully and embrace the Mystery of death, from one of the greatest writers in the field of death and dying. Also: **Who Dies?; Healing Into Life and Death; Guided Meditations, Explorations and Healings; others.**

Northrup, Christianne. **Women's Bodies, Women's Wisdom.** 1994, Bantam. A brilliant, comprehensive exploration of holistic women's health.

Siegel, Bernie. **Love, Medicine & Miracles.** 1986, HarperPerennial. Unconditional love is the most powerful stimulant of the immune system, according to this #1 best-seller and classic in the mind-body field.

Travis, John W. and Ryan, Regina Sara. **The Wellness Workbook, 2nd Ed.** 1988, Ten-Speed Press. A whole-systems approach to wellness, designed to help you take control of how you manage your energy.

Weil, Andrew. **8 Weeks to Optimum Health.** 1997, Fawcett. A practical plan of action for enhancing and protecting present and lifelong health. Also: **Spontaneous Healing,** many others.

Resources

The Center for Journal Therapy
1115 Grant Street #207 Denver, CO 80203
888-421-2298, in Colorado 303-986-6460
info@journaltherapy.com   www.journaltherapy.com
An international organization dedicated to making the healing art of journal writing accessible to all who desire self-directed change. Programs include home-study or residential intensive Instructor Certification Training to teach the *Journal to the Self* workshop. Advanced certification as a Wellness Specialist to facilitate *The Write Way to Wellness* curriculum is also available. A network of over 100 Certified Instructors teach journal workshops in many states, cities and regions in the US, Canada and New Zealand. The Center sponsors a week-long women's writing retreat each summer facilitated by Kay Adams, as well as various other workshops and seminars for the public with notables such as Deena Metzger, John Fox, Dana Reynolds and other guest faculty. Founder/Director Kathleen Adams also teaches and consults to mental health and healthcare professionals on therapeutic uses of writing in treatment. All programs are approved for continuing education for psychotherapists through the National Board for Certified Counselors, and some are also approved for continuing education for nurses.

The National Association for Poetry Therapy (NAPT)

www.poetrytherapy.org
An energetic, world-wide community of people who share a love for the use of language arts in growth and healing. Membership is multidisciplinary. Approximately 25% are mental health professionals, 25% doctors, nurses and physical healthcare professionals, 25% educators and librarians, 25% writers and poets. Credentialing program is available resulting in Certified Poetry Therapist (adult education/developmental level) or Registered Poetry Therapist (clinical level) designation. Dues $100/year. Publications include quarterly *Journal of Poetry Therapy* (Dr. Nicholas Mazza, Editor) and thrice-yearly *Museletter* (Linda Lanza, Editor). Annual conference is held in May each year.

The Judith K. Mahrer Scholarship Fund
c/o The National Association for Poetry Therapy Foundation

A scholarship fund to assist people in genuine financial need who desire training in poetry/journal therapy. All donations are fully tax-deductible. Mark checks "JKM Scholarship." Donations of $100 or more receive a set of "Healing Words" note cards. Applicants must send letter of request stating training desired and how training will be used.

The Wordsworth Center for Growth and Healing
7715 White Rim Terrace   Potomac MD 20854
301-983-3392 PegOHeller@aol.com
The Wordsworth Center offers three educational programs in poetry therapy, each of which is consistent with the training and supervision requirements for CPT or RPT credentials conferred by NAPT. Distance learning (home-study) programs available.Directed by poetry therapy pioneers Dr. Peggy Osna Heller and Dr. Ken Gorelick.

Healing Arts Books
12477 W. Cedar Dr #100
Lakewood CO 80228
303-716-5727   ccheal@aol.com, "ATTN: BOOKSTORE" in subject line
A full-service book/gift store which will order and ship any book in print, with highly personable and individualized service. Healing Arts Books stocks all the books listed in this bibliography.

LifeJournal Software
www.lifejournal.com
An excellent journal software program endorsed by Kay Adams, influenced by and compatible with the *Journal to the Self* approach. Download free trial version from the LifeJournal website, or order from www.journaltherapy.com/book/htm or on page 157. Requires Pentium or higher processor, CD ROM drive. Sorry, no Mac version presently available.

Sound Healers Association
P.O. Box 2240
Boulder, CO 80306
303-443-8181   800-246-9764   www.healingsounds.com
Sound healing seminars and sonic tools for transformation with Jonathan Goldman, sound healing pioneer, author of *Healing Sounds,* and creator of numerous award-winning recordings, including *Chakra Chants.* Jonathan provided the music for the companion *Write Way to Wellness Meditations* audio tape.

About the Author

Kathleen Adams, MA LPC is the founder/Director of The Center for Journal Therapy and the co-founder (with Mary Maynard, RN) of The Center for Healing and Change, both in Lakewood CO. She is the author of the best-selling *Journal to the Self: 22 Paths to Personal Growth* (1990, Warner Books), *The Way of the Journal, 2nd Ed.: A Journal Therapy Workbook for Healing* (1998, Sidran Press), and *Mightier Than the Sword: The Journal as a Path to Men's Self-Discovery* (currently out of print; ask about photocopied edition).

Kay is an approved provider of continuing education through the National Board of Certified Counselors, the Alcohol and Drug Abuse Division of the Colorado Department of Health, and the Colorado Nurses Association.

She is on the Executive Board of the National Association for Poetry Therapy and is President of the National Association for Poetry Therapy Foundation, a 501(c)(3) tax-exempt charitable/educational corporation. In 1996 she founded the Judith K. Mahrer Scholarship Fund in honor of the first National Coordinator of The Center for Journal Therapy. Kay was the recipient of NAPT's Distinguished Service Award for 1998.

Companion Products

All products may be ordered on-line from the CJT website, **www.journaltherapy.com/book/htm,** or by calling toll-free, 1-888-421-2998 (in Colorado, 303-986-6460). Alternatively, you may order from this page and fax to 303-985-3903 or mail to 1115 Grant Street, #207, Denver CO 80203.

The Write Way to Wellness Meditations. A companion audiotape to this workbook, with entrance meditations for the writing processes in this book. Background music by sound healer Jonathan Goldman. .... _____ @ $10 = $_____

The Write Way to Wellness: A Workbook for Healing and Change. Order additional copies of this workbook for friends and loved ones. Autographed to _____ .... _____ @ $19 = $_____

Special! Order *Write Way to Wellness Workbook* and *Meditations* tape together for only $25! Autographed to _____................................. _____ @ $25 = $_____

Journal to the Self. A warm guide to journal keeping as a rewarding path to greater self-awareness. Very reader-friendly. A classic work! Autographed to _____ .... _____ @ $14 = $_____

The Way of the Journal. In this well-designed workbook you'll learn fundamental journal skills to build confidence, clarity and results. Especially helpful for those in psychotherapy or recovery. Autographed to _____ .... _____ @ $19 = $_____

Journal to the Self Audio Workshop. This 5-tape set includes all four sessions of the popular workshop on which the best-selling book was based. Very interactive. Learn from master teacher Kay Adams in the privacy of your own home or office!.. _____ @ $95 = $_____

Journal to the Self Tote Bag in jade green with white lettering. Perfect for carrying books, journals, snacks. .... _____ @ $20 = $_____

LifeJournal Software. An excellent, very user-friendly way to keep your journal on computer. Separate templates for dream journal, regular journal, life log, daily mood/stress graph, much more! Requires PC, Pentium processor, CD Drive. Sorry, Mac version not available. .... _____ @ $40 = $_____

Colorado residents, add 6.3% tax ....TAX *(Colo only)* $_____
Shipping/handling ($5 up to $50, $6 up to $99, $7 over $100) ....SHIPPING $_____
TOTAL $_____

Name _____

Address _____

City_____ State_____ Zip _____

Phone _____ E-mail _____

Credit Card: ☐ MasterCard   ☐ Visa

Card #_____ Exp. Date _____ Signature _____

Blank Worksheets

 # My Self-Portrait

Today's Date _____   Start Time _____   End Time _____

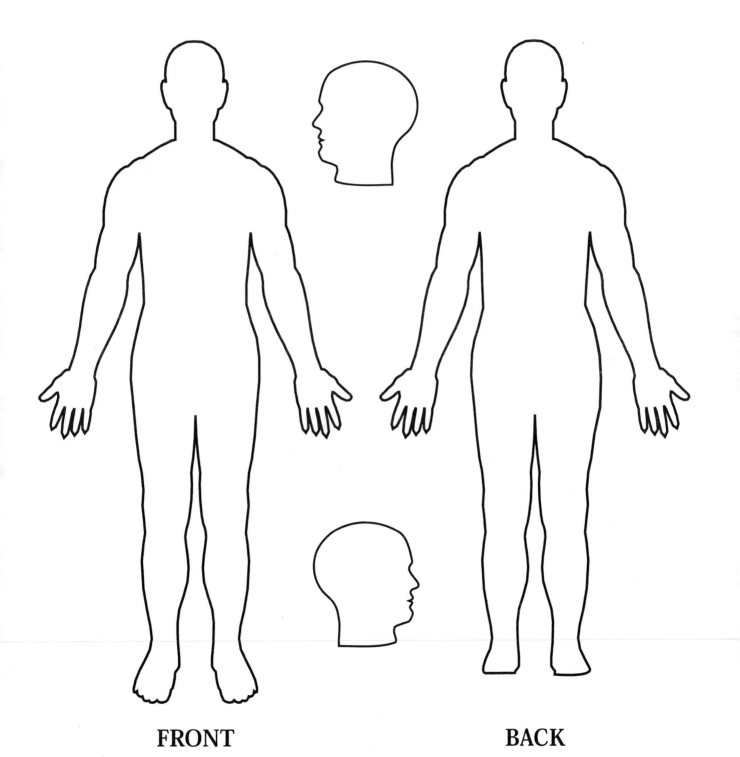

FRONT   **BACK**

My Health History

Birth	5	10

11	15	20

21	25	30

31	35	40

41	45	50

51	55	60

61	65	70

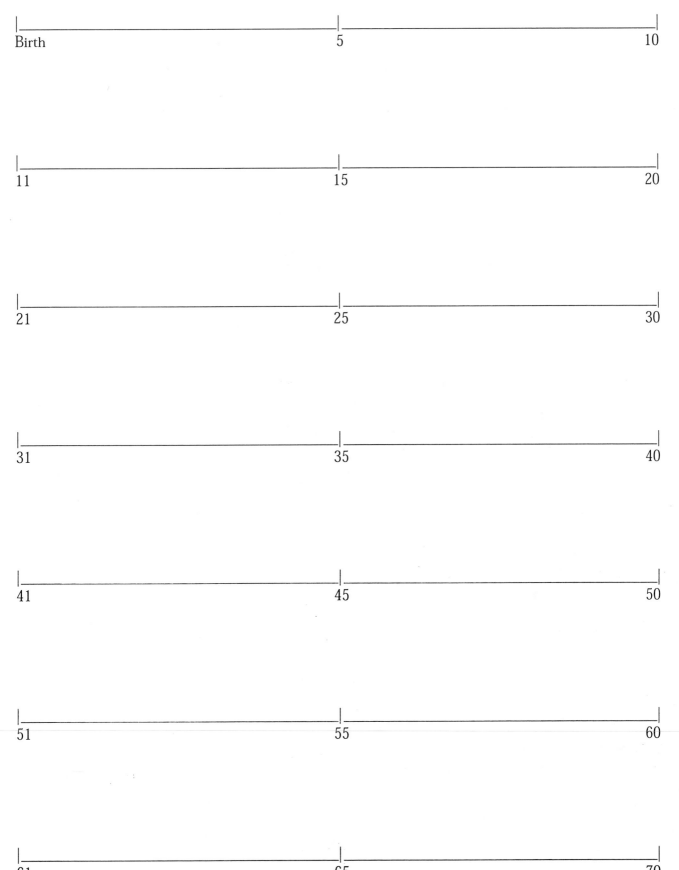

 **Relaxation Response Log**

Date _____

Date _____

Date _____

Date _____

Date _____

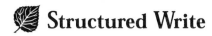 **Structured Write**

Today's date _____

The topic I want to explore is.......

The first thing that comes to mind.....

Beneath the surface I find......

I am disturbed or uncomfortable with......

I feel hopeful about.....

I would benefit from....

My next step is ....

Star Chart

for the week of _____

It takes 42 days to change a habit!

Task	Monday Date:	Tuesday Date:	Wednesday Date:	Thursday Date:	Friday Date:	Saturday Date:	Sunday Date:
How many times this week? _____							
How many times this week? _____							
How many times this week? _____							
How many times this week? _____							
How many times this week? _____							
How many times this week? _____							

AlphaPoem – Title: _____

A

B

C

D

E

F

G

H

I

J

K

L

M

N

O

P

Q

R

S

T

U

V

W

X

Y

Z

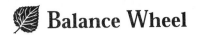 **Balance Wheel**

Today's Date _____   Start Time _____   End Time _____

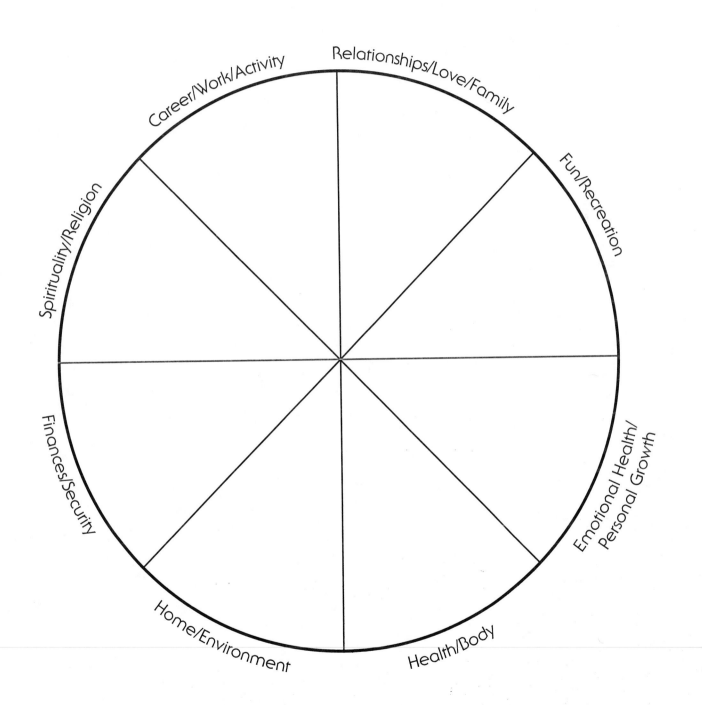

🍃 Applying Core Values

Today's Date _____   Start Time _____   End Time _____

A difficult or troublesome situation I am facing is

A brief synopsis of the situation is

If I applied my core value of _____ to this situation, then

If I applied my core value of _____ to this situation, then

If I applied my core value of _____ to this situation, then

 **Loss Lifeline**

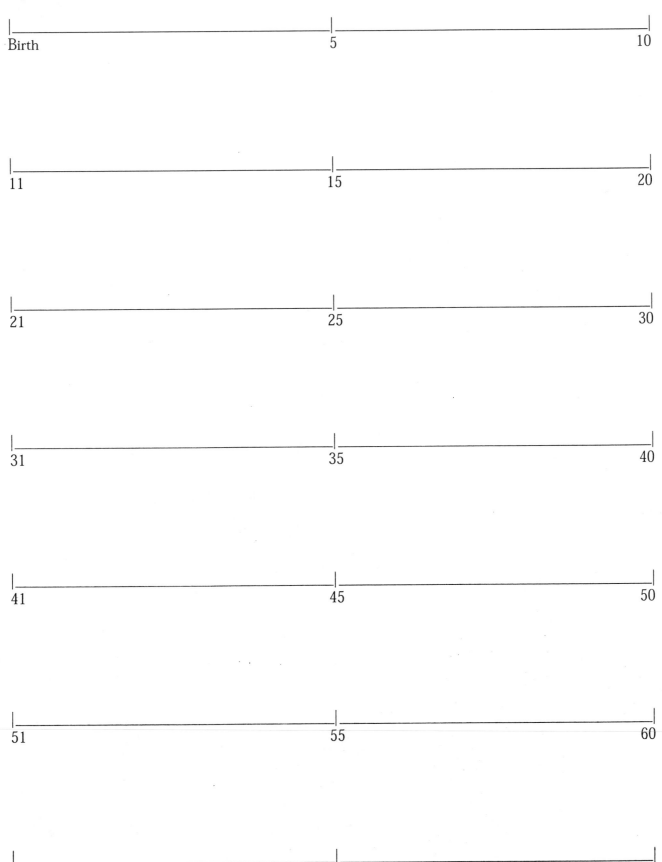

|
Birth   5   10

|
11   15   20

|
21   25   30

|
31   35   40

|
41   45   50

|
51   55   60

|
61   65   70

List of 100 _____

Today's Date _____   Start Time _____   End Time _____

1 _____	26 _____
2 _____	27 _____
3 _____	28 _____
4 _____	29 _____
5 _____	30 _____
6 _____	31 _____
7 _____	32 _____
8 _____	33 _____
9 _____	34 _____
10 _____	35 _____
11 _____	36 _____
12 _____	37 _____
13 _____	38 _____
14 _____	39 _____
15 _____	40 _____
16 _____	41 _____
17 _____	42 _____
18 _____	43 _____
19 _____	44 _____
20 _____	45 _____
21 _____	46 _____
22 _____	47 _____
23 _____	48 _____
24 _____	49 _____
25 _____	50 _____

51 _____

52 _____

53 _____

54 _____

55 _____

56 _____

57 _____

58 _____

59 _____

60 _____

61 _____

62 _____

63 _____

64 _____

65 _____

66 _____

67 _____

68 _____

69 _____

70 _____

71 _____

72 _____

73 _____

74 _____

75 _____

76 _____

77 _____

78 _____

79 _____

80 _____

81 _____

82 _____

83 _____

84 _____

85 _____

86 _____

87 _____

88 _____

89 _____

90 _____

91 _____

92 _____

93 _____

94 _____

95 _____

96 _____

97 _____

98 _____

99 _____

100 _____